PEACE TOGETHER

PEACE TOGETHER

A Vision of Christian Pacifism

Editor:
CLIVE BARRETT

James Clarke & Co
Cambridge

James Clarke & Co
7 All Saints' Passage
Cambridge CB2 3LS

British Library cataloguing in Publication Data

Peace together: a vision of Christian pacifism.
1. Pacifism – Religious aspects – Christianity
I. Barrett, Clive
261.8′73   BT736.6
ISBN 0–227–67893–1

First published 1987 by James Clarke & Co

Typeset in Monophoto Baskerville by
Vision Typesetting, Manchester

Printed in Great Britain by
The Guernsey Press Co. Ltd.,
Guernsey, Channel Islands

Dedicated to the men and women who have recovered the gospel of peace for the Church in the past fifty years and all who are working today to encourage Christians to take their peacemaking responsibilities seriously in the next fifty years.

Contents

PART 3   CHANGING THE WORLD

PART 4   A GLIMPSE OF HEAVEN

PART 5   CONCLUSION

APPENDICES

Notes on the Contributors

George Appleton was formerly Archbishop in Jerusalem. He is a member of APF.

John Austin Baker is Bishop of Salisbury and Chairman of the 'Church and the Bomb' working party.

Clive Barrett is a priest in Yorkshire and a member of APF.

Jenny Barrett was formerly a fieldworker for the Christian Movement for Peace. She is a member of APF.

David Bleakley is General Secretary of the Irish Council of the Churches and a member of FOR.

Barbara Eggleston is National Co-ordinator of the Christian Campaign for Nuclear Disarmament.

John Ferguson was formerly Principal of Selly Oak College. He is a member of FOR.

Valerie Flessati was formerly General Secretary of Pax Christi. She is currently researching the history of the Catholic peace movement.

John M. Gessell was formerly Professor of Ethics at the University of the South, Tennessee. He is a member of EPF.

Bruce Kent is Vice-Chair of the Campaign for Nuclear Disarmament. He is a member of Pax Christi.

Sara Maitland is a feminist writer.

James O'Connell is Professor of Peace Studies at Bradford University.

Paul Oestreicher is Director of International Ministry at Coventry Cathedral. He is a member of APF.

Clare Prangley is Chairperson of the British Section of Pax Christi.

Christopher Rowland is Dean of Jesus College, Cambridge and a member of APF.

Donald Soper was formerly President of the Methodist Conference. He is a member of FOR.

Gordon Wilson is Organiser of the Week of Prayer for World Peace and Chairman of APF.

The contributors are all 'pacifist, or sympathetic to Christian pacifism'. Each contributor is responsible for her/his own work only. No acceptance of the views expressed by other contributors should be in any way implied.

Abbreviations Used

APF   Anglican Pacifist Fellowship
CND   Campaign for Nuclear Disarmament
EPF   Episcopal Peace Fellowship
FOR   Fellowship of Reconciliation

Introduction
Clive Barrett

' "The question is," said Alice, "whether you *can* make words mean so many different things." '

Certain words in the English language speak of what are regarded as good things. They leave a feeling of warmth, satisfaction. Democracy is one, freedom another. The fact that no two groups seem to mean the same when they use such words is immaterial. They are clearly speaking of good things.

Other words describe what are generally regarded as bad things. Marxist is one, pacifist another. They are contemptuous labels used by the comfortable of those who just hint that everything in everybody's garden might not be quite so rosy. You don't need to recite *Das Kapital* to be labelled Marxist, just ask awkward questions. In Dom Helder Camara's words, 'When I give food to the poor, they call me a saint. When I ask why the poor have no food, they call me a communist.'

It is the same with pacifism. Anyone who questions whether massive unilateral nuclear rearmament by Britain makes any sense in a world with enough weaponry to destroy itself several times over is dismissed as pacifist. (On that basis, even the SDP, whose very existence came about because of their trust in nuclear weapons and their fear of genuine disarmament, would be described as pacifist!)

Even amongst those who call themselves pacifist there are a variety of approaches:

(a) Some are prepared to seek actively a situation where non-resistance is applicable. (Matt. 5.38–9: 'You have heard that it was said, "An eye for an eye and a tooth for a tooth." But I say to you, Do not resist one who is evil.')

1

(b) Many would reject all forms of violence that seek (or do not rule out) injury to others, without rejecting other forms of force, such as non-violent resistance. (Violence to property, for example, is of a different order from violence to human beings made in God's image.)

(c) Similarly, lesser forms of violence may not necessarily be rejected by those who emphasise the sixth commandment, 'Thou shalt not kill' (Exod. 20.13). What matters is that it is not possible to love one's enemies (Matt. 5.44) and also to kill them.

These are but a few of the different varieties of pacifism. Most of these positions are reflected at some stage in this volume. Together with the insults of anti-pacifists, it is clear that the answer to Alice's question is, 'Yes'. Unless terms are defined, it becomes meaningless to talk about them. Perhaps the most useful definition of the term 'pacifist' is that based on the statement made by members of the Anglican Pacifist Fellowship, who, believing that the Christian faith 'involves the complete repudiation of modern war, pledge [themselves] to renounce war and all preparation to wage war and to work for the construction of Christian peace in the world.'

REPUDIATION OF MODERN WARFARE

This definition includes the brands of pacifism indicated above. It does not necessarily imply a condemnation of participation in past wars. There *is* a strong pacifist tradition to be affirmed (see my later chapter), but there are those who feel that military opposition to Nazism, for example, was appropriate who nonetheless believe that in the nuclear age, any warfare or military threat (whether nuclear or not) is both foolish and wrong. This definition includes all whose pacifism is based on the horrific nature of modern warfare. Even Pope John Paul II, at Coventry in 1982, made the declaration, 'The horror of modern warfare, whether nuclear or not, makes it totally unacceptable as a means of settling differences between nations.' Pacifists would continue by saying that they therefore want nothing to do with it and that they want neither their church nor their nation to have anything to do with it.

RENOUNCE WAR AND ALL PREPARATION TO WAGE WAR

In a complex and interwoven society, it is neither possible nor desirable to opt out of community life. Pacifism is *not* about keeping one's own conscience clean; it is not possible and to that extent we do live in a 'fallen' world. However, there has been a tradition (akin to monasticism) of individuals witnessing to values neglected by the rest of society. Pacifism has often been acknowledged as an acceptable vocation for a few, provided they do not stop others getting on with the fighting. One of the dangers of concentrating on an individual's pledge of pacifism is that it tends to reinforce the vocational misconception.

It is a misconception. Modern warfare is total warfare. We are all in the front line. Under the evil policies of deterrence, preparations for mass murder are made on our behalf and we are all threatened with the same fate. The vested interests of the arms manufacturers and others have made most negotiations a charade; overkill is ignored and the arms race flourishes whilst millions die of hunger. The holocaust is *now* for those whose resources have been appropriated by rich nations preaching deterrence and fear.

In such a context, the need is urgent for the universal Church to recognise the evils of our age and to unequivocally renounce war and all preparation to wage war. In particular, the established Church could be proclaiming to government that renouncing war is not only the only acceptable moral policy, but also practical, even essential, politics.

WORK FOR THE CONSTRUCTION OF CHRIST'S PEACE IN THE WORLD

Pacifism is more than conscientious objection in time of war. Etymologically, it indicates peacemaking. For Christians, it means being wary of those claiming peace when there is no peace, but rather the fear induced by deterrence and the hunger induced by the arms race. For those who believe that 'perfect love casts out fear' (1 John 4.18), it means being led by the Holy Spirit to work for that justice and harmony for all of God's people that is at the heart of true peace. Pacifism is more than intellectual assent to an idea. It is a vision for living.

PEACE TOGETHER

Making *Peace Together* are a collection of writers from a wide variety of denominations, perspectives and backgrounds. They provide the vision with a breadth, a richness. One of the features of Christian peacemaking is its ability to unite those whom history has drawn apart.

The book falls into three categories: the basis, the issues and the practice.

When making moral decisions, Christians turn especially to scripture, tradition and prayer to inform their consciences. Here lies the basis of the Christian pacifist vision.

It is easy to hold such a philosophy when things are comfortable, but what about situations of injustice and conflict? Views are given by those well used to situations of conflict. 'Peace, peace, to the far and to the near, says the Lord' (Isa. 57.19).

Pressure of space has led to some omissions. Apologies are due to David Taylor of APF's sister organisation in New Zealand. The greatest lack is of a comprehensive treatment of the exciting renewal of Christian pacifism in the twentieth century. The Society of Friends deserve deeper treatment. The philosophy of the Peace Tax Campaign, the conversion of arms industries to peaceful use, the role of the United Nations and the fundamental relationship between peace and world development (not least, the work of the Campaign Against the Arms Trade) could all have been more fully explored. Part 3 is thus but a selection of the many aspects of living the vision of peace.

Peace Together promotes a theory and practice that is central to the Christian gospel, yet has so often been neglected by the Church. The vision of Christian pacifism needs to be accepted and lived by the Church as a matter of urgency. It is the only alternative to the evil of modern warfare. 'I have set before you life and death, blessing and curse; therefore choose life, that you and your descendants may live' (Deut. 30.19).

Or to put it another way, ' "The question is," said Humpty Dumpty, "which is to be master – that's all." '

1

THE

FOUNDATIONS

What exactly is Christian pacifism? This substantive section explores its basis by considering the meaning of peace and the biblical, historical, theological and spiritual roots of the Christian pacifist case.

The Meaning of Peace
Christopher Rowland

I

IT is easy to be sentimental about the word 'peace', an attitude which is reinforced by prevailing use of some of the New Testament passages in which the word occurs. Taken out of context, phrases like 'we have peace with God through our Lord Jesus Christ' (Rom. 5.1) and 'grace and peace . . . to you' (1 Pet. 1.2) suggest an atmosphere of calm and tranquillity which, in fact, contrasts with other aspects of the language and imagery of the Bible where judgement and conflict seem to be to the fore. A writer like Paul, from whom these words are taken, does not give an impression of having lived a peaceful life as an apostle of Jesus Christ, either personally or socially. Conflict, misunderstanding and tribulation seem to be never far from his mind as he put pen to paper. Therefore, we need to take care when examining the subject of peace in the Bible that we do not concentrate only on those passages which speak of peace or use the words *shālôm* and *eirene*. To do so would be to ignore the thrust of the biblical witness and distort our understanding of the context in which those words were used. To treat the subject adequately, we need to have some understanding of the context and that, in my view, means the hope for the future.

For most biblical writers, peace was rarely a reality and, more frequently, a goal still to be achieved. As such, it was always difficult to characterise the present situation of individual and community as being one of peace; that was something to be looked forward to. The politics of Israel's history supports this view. For much of the 500 years preceding the birth of Jesus, Jews in Palestine were under the control of foreign nations. Thus

7

the true peace in which God and his people would be regarded as Lord and paradigm for the nations of the world, respectively, was never realised. Even those times of political autonomy saw protest movements arising against imperfect claims to fulfilment of God's purposes. To speak in this way is to recognise that peace is above all an eschatological event, though not necessarily for that reason unattainable under God in this world. Jews and early Christians did not despair of the establishment of a reign of peace and justice on earth. Passages like Isaiah 11 speak in glowing terms about the harmony of humanity and nature in the Messianic age. The longing for a reign of peace varied according to the circumstances in which the people of God found themselves, but there was always a realistic expectation that God's world might experience 'the peace of God, which passes all understanding' (Phil. 4.7) when the reign of God was finally established on earth.

It is a mark of the development of the Christian doctrine of hope, that the main thrust of it has concentrated on the fate of the individual at death and the hope of heaven, hereafter. The words, 'Bring us, O Lord God, at our last awakening into the house and gate of heaven', beautifully summarise the dominant view of the Christian hope. Those Christians who have wanted to say more about hope and change for this world, have had to struggle with this pervasive view that the form of this world cannot be radically changed, and that in speaking of the Kingdom of God, Christians mean a world beyond this one. The problem with this view is that it sits ill with ancient Jewish and Christian views of hope. It is a fact that the establishment of the reign of God on earth was commonplace within Christianity for the first 200 years of its existence. Similarly, the dominant Jewish expectation, which in turn influenced the views of the first Christians, looked forward to the fulfilment of those Old Testament prophecies which speak of a period of righteousness and peace in the reign of the Messiah.

Today, many Christians are recognising the deep roots that this kind of expectation has within the Christian, as well as the Jewish, tradition. Also, they note the spiritualisation of key terms like 'redemption', which in Christian discourse has so often been linked with the release of the individual soul, rather than the liberation of a community; a meaning which is dominant in the Old Testament antecedents of the term. It has been frequently quoted, in recent years, by those who have sought to stress the centrality of the 'good news for the poor' in the proclamation of Jesus. The programmatic statement in Luke 4.18ff is a reiteration of the covenant demands of God for his people and the prophetic hopes for this world. Jesus tells his hearers that those hopes are being fulfilled, something which the story of Jesus in Luke's Gospel seeks to demonstrate (Luke 7.16). Thus it is not the case that contemporary Christians who stress the compatibility of the gospel with radical change are importing a view which is at odds with the gospel. Those who have sought to point out the link between the squandering of resources on the production of weapons of destruction and the impoverishment of millions of our fellow men and women are giving voice to the incompatibility of particular courses of action with God's purposes for humanity, firmly rooted in the biblical tradition itself. Even if we have no right to assert the superiority of our view of the tradition over that of some of our ancestors in the faith, we can say that we are rediscovering elements within our tradition which, however open to abuse they may be, need to be heard and used by those who wish to promote the peace of God, who is as concerned with this implementation at the political as at the individual level.

Unfortunately, we do not know as much as we would like about Jewish beliefs and practices in Jesus' day to be certain that there was a uniform expectation about the future. Even if there was, it is quite clear that there were significant differences in the ways in which different groups viewed the means whereby that age of peace would come about. Thus at one extreme we have the Zealots who, like the heroes of the biblical story, believed that it was the responsibility of the Elect to take up the sword and act as agents of God's purposes in liberating the holy land and people. For others, there was a more sanguine approach. The Sadducees accepted the Roman rule in Judea, probably with considerable reservations, as a means of guaranteeing the service of God in the Temple. Better the privations of Roman rule than the deprivation of cult and privilege which eschatological revolution might bring about. The Pharisees were concerned with holiness, also. But whereas the Essenes had to go out into the wilderness in complete separation, they were anxious to maintain sufficient leeway to provide for that space to be a holy people, a nation of priests, by maintaining ritual purity, full sabbath observance and proper tithing arrangements. Provided that this was maintained, no action need be taken to change the status quo, though there was, clearly, a profound hope that this would be done in the day of the coming Kingdom. God's time was best; he would inaugurate the eschatological process; and it was for the Elect to wait upon his will.

II

These general points need to be made because they serve as a backdrop to the interpretation of a saying which has long caused perplexity to Christians: 'Do you think that I have come to give peace on earth? No, I tell you, but rather division' (Luke 12.51). Space prevents a full discussion of this verse; but its implications should not be lost. Jesus' presence and message have the effect of *provoking conflict*, rather than bringing about immediate peace and reconciliation. If one pauses to think about this only briefly, the reasons are not really difficult to understand. All commentators on the gospels are agreed that Jesus came to proclaim and perhaps also inaugurate the eschatological hope of the Kingdom of God. In so doing, he was claiming the near fulfilment of the long-established hopes of Judaism. The expectation of such a Messianic age itself presupposes that the present order is unsatisfactory and contrasts unfavourably with what is promised. That would present a problem if it could be guaranteed that all would gladly accept the Messiah when he came. But the story of Messianic movements in the day of Jesus indicates that the fate of Jesus was not untypical of others who proclaimed the imminence of God's deliverance. There were always those who refused to deny the value of the present order in favour of an undefined implementation of various hopes for change, and others who, for various reasons, were unpersuaded of the validity of the claims of the Messiah when he arrived on the scene. It was, after all, a momentous thing to accept the fact that the Messiah had arrived and to implement the consequences of that acceptance. Consequently, it should come as no surprise to us that the claims of a Galilean prophet met with a mixed response. The crowds heard him gladly; but there were many in positions of authority who thought that his activity was less about the establishment of God's kingdom (Luke 11.20) and more about the unleashing of the powers of the evil empire (Mark 3.22). A conflict emerges between the proclaimer and agent of change and those who, for whatever reasons, reject the message. The goal of the reign of God is peace. But how will that goal be achieved? The painful fact is that, in the face of opposition, there will be suffering, not least for those who stand firm by the conviction of the coming of God's reign in Jesus.

It was that conviction of the Messiahship of Jesus and the peace and righteousness attending that claim which, in fact, led to tribulation for the one time persecutor of the people of the way, Saul of Tarsus. Paul perceived that peace was not merely an eschatological goal, but in some sense, however partial, could be glimpsed as a present reality by those who followed the Messiah. While there may have been a false sense of peace and security prevalent in a world which assumed that Roman might was invincible (1 Thess. 5.2), the members of the Body of Christ could taste peace and reconciliation in the Messiah, through the indwelling Spirit (Gal. 3.26ff; 5.22). It was not the case that present tribulation and conflict were dissipated thereby; for, as Paul himself constantly reiterates, it is necessary to push on to achieve the ultimate goal. The balance between what the follower of Jesus the Messiah may perceive here and now and what is still to come in the future is a central feature of Paul's thought. It is always tempting to suppose that a sentimental attachment to inward peace now can enable the disciple to escape from the tension inherent in the espousal of an unfulfilled, and yet partially realised, hope. To think of the peace which Christ brings as solely, or even mainly, a present reality is to diminish the central importance of that overall framework of future hope in the New Testament as well as the Old Testament. Certainly, the peace of God may be glimpsed in the present, not least in the fellowship of the Messianic group. But that conviction that true peace has arrived for the individual or the small group must never usurp the conviction that the Spirit is only a pledge of a greater glory to be revealed (Rom. 8.22; 2 Cor. 1.22; 2 Cor. 5.20). In the understanding of Christian theology, there is no doubt that the difficulties and perplexities posed by the world around have tempted Christians to confine themselves to personal and inward peace. That is unrealistic and impoverishes the power and the scope of the gospel.

III

It has become commonplace in Christian theology that it is not the Christian's role to protest at his or her suffering, thereby following the example of Christ. The justification is most clearly set out in 1 Peter, which seeks to persuade Christians to accept suffering because they are Christians, on the basis of the example of Christ. At the end of 1 Peter 2, the Suffering Servant passage from Isaiah 53 is quoted and Jesus is held out as a model of the passive acceptance of one's lot which has characterised so many Christian attitudes to suffering and injustice. It is a superficially plausible position, which has gained its support by repetition in word and deed over the centuries. Yet its recommendation of Christian passivity as the form of pacifism must be challenged. The gospels themselves hardly portray Jesus as one who was the unwilling and passive victim; or, at least, a full reading of them does not support such a view. If we were to concentrate on Jesus' attitude on the night of his arrest and trial, the emphasis on passivity as a model would seem to be confirmed. But we have to ask what led him into this predicament. Was he a victim of circumstances totally beyond his control? To such questions the gospel narratives give a resoundingly negative answer. 'My time has not yet come', the Johannine Jesus says to his brothers (7.6). That is a view which is echoed in the other gospels. The Lucan Jesus 'set his face to go to Jerusalem' (9.51), 'for it cannot be that a prophet should perish away from Jerusalem' (13.33). In Mark and Matthew, we read of Jesus speaking of the necessity of the Son of Man suffering and being rejected in Jerusalem. The narratives do not portray an assassination of Jesus in Galilee, even if such attempts were made or contemplated from time to time (Mark 3.6 and John 8.59). Rather, Jesus deliberately sets out to go to Jerusalem; and what is more, makes a public spectacle in the Temple precincts. Apart from the Gospel of John, where the Triumphal Entry is portrayed as a spontaneous reaction of Jesus to the eschatological enthusiasm of the crowd, the Synoptic Gospels portray the event as deliberately organised by Jesus. Just as it is a distortion to extract these events from the whole fabric of the passion story and suppose that they indicate Jesus' participation in violent revolutionary change in the manner of the Jewish freedom fighters, so it is equally wrong to ignore the wider context which led to the death of Jesus, and to interpret that death merely in the light of those references to silence and passivity at the trial. An acceptance of the dynamism of the message, with its political and social implications, is not easily squared with a picture of Jesus as one who meekly accepted his fate. This issue is intimately linked with the important question of means and ends. To assert that, in general terms, Jesus' goal of a reign of righteousness may not have been too far removed from those of his contemporaries, is not to minimise the gulf which existed between them over the means whereby that reign of peace was to be brought about.

Paul's insistence on 'not I but Christ' should remind us that he thought of his own life as an apostle as a constant imitation of Christ and his way in the circumstances of his day (1 Cor. 11.1; 2 Cor. 4.10). That imitation did not mean the ready acceptance of suffering, for Paul's career is a story of provocation leading to conflict in the name of the gospel. The Cross and Resurrection of Jesus is an act of ultimate significance. Reconciliation and peace with God have been initiated, but the time when God will be all in all is still in the future (1 Cor. 15.20ff; Eph. 1.10). There can be no room for easy talk about reconciliation when the circumstances which can make that reconciliation impossible are still in force. Even at the level of the individual, there is no relief from that tension (Rom. 7). Justification by faith can take place; salvation, peace and revelation of the ultimate righteousness of God throughout the cosmos are still to come. Paul, the apostle of good news, still has to carry on that mission, which will involve him in the same rejection, tribulation and suffering as his master. While he never recommends violent retaliation to the persecution which is initiated, the pursuit of the eschatological peace demands both conformity to that attitude of non-violence and also acceptance of the fact that a challenge has to be made to all that stands in the way of the fulfilment of that peace. To proclaim and live the gospel will involve us all in the same protests and witness which characterised the careers of both Jesus and Paul.

The Biblical Basis of Pacifism

John Ferguson

CREATION

THE creation stories show a world teeming with living creatures. The animals are at peace with one another, feeding on the plants which are there fore their sustenance. Humankind, male and female, are given the highest place in the Peaceable Kingdom, and man co-operates with God in the creative work of giving names to the animals.

It is with the Fall that violence enters the world, an event epitomised in the story of Cain and Abel (Gen. 4). We may not forget that we live in a fallen world, a world which is patently not as God intends it to be. We may not forget, either, the world as God wills it. The first fact about creation is that it is good; the second, that it is marred. The first fact about human beings is that we are made in God's image; the second, that we are fallen. We must keep before us, as the prophets did, the vision of the Peaceable Kingdom restored, where the wolf lives with the sheep and the leopard lies down with the kid, and none shall hurt or destroy (Isa. 11.6–9). So too, Hosea proclaims a new covenant of God with the animals, birds and reptiles, declaring that God will put an end to war, so that all living creatures may lie down without fear (Hos. 2.18).

THE DELIVERANCE FROM EGYPT

Although the earlier migration from Mesopotamia no doubt contains an authentic folk-memory, the solid history of the Jewish people and the beginning of their distinctive religion coincide in the deliverance from Egypt under the leadership of Moses and the subsequent covenant on Mount Sinai. 'I am the Lord your God, who brought you up out of the land of Egypt' (Ps. 81.10). The deliverance was a military act, and the triumph-song of Moses and the Israelites proclaimed, 'The Lord is a warrior' (Exod. 15.3) and rejoiced over the destruction of Pharaoh's army. Only later does a different attitude prevail. One Rabbi told how the angels wanted to raise a paean over the engulfed Egyptian army, but God cried 'What? The work of my hands is drowning in the sea and you would chant hymns before me!' (*Sanhedrin* 396)

So too, the entry into Canaan was accomplished by a warfare and massacre which were regarded as blessed by God, though it should not be forgotten that when Joshua met the captain of the Lord's army, and asked 'Are you for us or for our enemies?', the implicit answer was 'Neither' (Josh. 5.13–14). At the end of his life, Joshua is recorded as putting into the mouth of God a conspectus of Israelite history (Josh. 24.2–13), starting from Terah and Abraham, accepting God's own direct responsibility for the destruction of the Egyptians, and going on to say that he, the Lord, destroyed the Amorites for the sake of Israel, saved Israel from Moab and delivered Jericho into the hands of the Israelites. 'I gave you a land on which you did not toil and cities you did not build; and you live in them and eat from vineyards and olive groves you did not plant' (Josh. 24.13).

Behind this lies a view of God. The Israelites believed in the almighty power of God. All that happened happened by his will. If Pharaoh's heart was hardened, God hardened it; if God had not hardened it, it could not have been hardened (Exod. 9.12, etc.). If Israel conquered in battle, it was through the will and power of the Lord. Israel did – sometimes – conquer in battle; so God is 'the Lord strong and mighty, the Lord mighty in battle' (Ps. 24.8), 'the Lord of hosts' (1 Sam. 17.45, etc.). And when Israel did not conquer, this too was by God's will, in punishment for their disobedience and sin. He was still the Lord mighty in battle, but he placed his mightiness on the side of Israel's opponents.

THE HISTORY OF ISRAEL AS MILITARY HISTORY

The Israelites were a military people; in this they were no different from others. The Book of Judges begins with the

enquiry as to which tribe should attack the Canaanites first
(1.1). So the men of Judah slaughter 10,000 Canaanites and
Perizzites, mutilate a prisoner of war, sack Jerusalem. Deborah
was prominent in raising an Israelite army (4.4–10), though the
later Rabbis liked to interpret her aggressive words spiritually
(*Yoma* 23a, *Shabbat* 88b, *Gittin* 36b). Gideon was called by the
Lord to free Israel from the Midianites (Judg. 6.14). Jephthah
was a great soldier, chosen by the leaders of Israel to fight the
Ammonites (11.1–11). Samson claimed to kill a thousand men
with an ass's jawbone (15.16).

So the catalogue goes on. The Ark of the Lord represents the
very presence of God in the campaigns (1 Sam. 4.1–11). Saul is
anointed, admittedly against Samuel's judgement, as a war-
leader. David goes out against Goliath 'in the name of the Lord
of hosts, the God of the army of Israel' (1 Sam. 17.45). Hezekiah
stood up to Sennacherib in the confidence that, although the
Assyrians had human strength, 'we have the Lord our God to
help us and to fight our battles' (2 Chr. 32.8), and the
deliverance from Sennacherib was a classic example of the
Lord's action (2 Kgs. 19.1–36; 2 Chr. 32.1–23; Isa. 37.1–38). It
remains an ambiguous story, for it was a violent deliverance, but
it was not carried out by the armies of Judah. So too, we find
Nehemiah restoring the walls of Jerusalem, with half his men
building and half standing to arms, in the faith that 'God will
fight for us' (Neh. 4.20); so too, Judas Maccabaeus, as he faced
the Greek armies, recalled the deliverance from Egypt and
asserted that 'there is one who saves and liberates Israel' (1
Macc. 4.8–11).

But God did not save in face of Roman arms in AD 66–70 or
132–5. Those who took the sword perished by the sword.

OTHER ELEMENTS IN THE TRADITION

There are other elements even within the Old Testament.
First, the Lord is the God of Israel. But he is not a mere
projection of their being onto the infinite; he is linked to them by
a covenant relationship. This meant that what he was to Israel,
he might be to all people. So the captain of the Lord's army was
neither for Israel nor for her enemies (Josh. 5.13–14). So Amos
declared that the Israelites were no more (and no less) to God
than the Negroes of Cush, or their traditional enemies, the
Philistines and Aramaeans (Amos 9.7). From this comes the

vision that all the peoples of the earth shall be united in God's kingdom of peace (Isa. 2.2; Mic. 4.1).

Second, the covenant was from the first associated with a moral code, which we call the Ten Commandments. The Lord demanded righteousness of his people and, as the years passed, warfare and violence were seen to stand under judgement. So Simeon and Levi used treacherous violence to avenge the honour of their sister Dinah and, on his death-bed, Jacob cursed them for it (Gen. 34.1–31; 49.5–7). So David, the heroic soldier-king, was not allowed to build the Temple because he had been a warrior and had shed blood (1 Chr. 28.2–3). So Jehu, with Elisha backing him, massacred the apostate house of Ahab and the Baal-worshippers, seemingly with the Lord's blessing (2 Kgs. 9–10), but the prophet Hosea, also in the Lord's name, saw these self-same actions as a crime (Hos. 1.4).

Third, there is a strong tradition that the people of God should rely on him, rather than on military power.

> Some boast of chariots, and some of horses;
> but we boast of the name of the Lord our God.
> They will collapse and fall;
> but we shall rise and stand upright.   (Ps. 20.7–8)

So Isaiah quoted God as saying, 'Come back, keep peace, and you will be safe; in stillness and in staying quiet, there lies your strength' (Isa. 30.15). The great deliverances from Pharaoh and Sennacherib create considerable theological problems, but they offer no encouragement to exponents of military defence; their lesson is rather that God is perfectly capable of looking after his own without their help. So when Nebuchadrezzar was seen as a threat, Jeremiah proclaimed that it was the Lord's will that he should be a world-ruler and that Judah should submit; the alternative was destruction (Jer. 27.17). It is important to see that this is presented as religious obedience, not pragmatic calculation. So Zechariah declared 'Not by might, nor by power, but by my Spirit, says the Lord of hosts' (Zech. 4.6). It is notable that the feast of Hannukah celebrates the Maccabean deliverance, but that this Zechariah passage is appointed for reading.

Fourth, there is a stress upon compassion. The Aramaeans were trying to capture Elisha. They were deluded and led into Samaria. The King of Israel cried excitedly: 'My father, shall I smite them? Shall I smite them?' But Elisha told him to let them eat and drink and return to their master. 'And Aramaean raids on Israel ceased.' (2 Kgs. 6.8–23). On another occasion, the northern kingdom had committed an act of aggression against Judah and taken a large number of prisoners. A Samaritan prophet named Oded insisted that the prisoners of war be fed, clothed, medically cared for and returned home, with transport provided for the unfit (2 Chr. 28.1–15). Most notable of all is the story of Jonah, and the Lord withholding the threatened destruction from Nineveh. 'Should not I be sorry for the great city of Nineveh, with its hundred and twenty thousand who cannot tell their right hand from their left, and also much cattle?' (Jonah 4.11). For the Lord is 'a god compassionate and gracious, long-suffering, ever constant and true, maintaining constancy to thousands, forgiving iniquity, rebellion and sin, and not sweeping the guilty clean away (Exod. 34.6–7).

Fifth, we must not forget the extraordinary transvaluation of normally accepted standards in the songs of the Suffering Servant, and especially in Isaiah 52.13–53.12. The Servant is exalted by God because, instead of meeting violence with violence, he has elected to suffer for others. There are complicated issues of interpretation, not least for Christians. Christians see this prophecy as having its fulfilment in Jesus, who made it his own. But it must be seen also in its historical context. The Servant seems at one point to be Israel, who thus is called to suffer rather than to meet violence with violence, at others to be an individual, perhaps, but not certainly, King Jehoiachin, who went to exile and death rather than see his city sacked. Be that as it may, the transvaluation is there.

SHĀLÔM

Throughout the Old Testament, there is a commitment to peace.

> Let me hear the words of the Lord:
> are they not words of peace,
> peace to his people and his loyal servants
> and to all who turn and trust in him?
> Deliverance is near to those who worship him,
> so that glory may dwell in our land.
> Love and fidelity have come together;
> justice and peace join hands.   (Ps. 85.8–10)

Peace, *shālôm*, means freedom from war (Judg. 4.17; 1 Kgs. 4.24; 5.12; Eccles. 3.8). The Lord is a god who does away with war. 'From end to end of the earth he stamps out war' (Ps. 48.9). He brings disarmament, breaking the instruments of war (ibid.; Hos. 2.18; Zech. 9.10) or transforming them into constructive tools (Isa. 2.4; Mic. 4.3). The King will speak peaceably to every nation (Zech. 9.10).

But the word itself means more than this. It comes from a root meaning 'wholeness'. It is well-being or harmony for all people in community. It is the proper condition of human beings in relationship with one another, as they greet with peace and part with peace. It includes health, prosperity, long life and fullness of life – all those things which half of humanity still conspicuously lack today. To boast the absence of war while this is true is to cry, ' "Peace, peace," when there is no peace' (Jer. 6.14). Micah spells out the meaning of *shālôm*: 'Nation shall not lift up sword against nation or train for war; weapons are beaten into agricultural implements and each man shall dwell under his own vine and fig tree, undisturbed' (Mic. 4.3–4).

THE CHRISTIAN UNDERSTANDING OF THE OLD TESTAMENT

It is impossible to escape from the fact of war in the Old Testament, or the characterisation of the Lord as a god of battles. It must, however, be equally firmly stated that Christians are members of the New Covenant, not the Old. Again and again in the Sermon on the Mount (Matt. 5.1–7.29) Jesus says, 'You have learned that our forefathers were told. . . . But what I tell you is this.' When he says, 'You have learned that they were told "Love your neighbour, hate your enemy." But what I tell you is this: Love your enemies' (Matt. 5.43–4), he is laying upon us a new way, different from war. To fulfil and complete the law, he had sometimes to annul it (Eph. 2.15). For the Christian, the Old Testament is incomplete; if it were not so, there would have been no need for a New Covenant.

Some Christians may wish to say that the Old Testament was authoritative for the people to whom it was originally given. They in their generation were justified in their wars, but we are a new people given over to peace: something similar was said by the early Church Fathers. Others will find it impossible to say that God changes and will rather say that the Old Testament represents an often profound, but still imperfect, understanding of God. Some will see within the scriptures a growth in understanding. The great prophets show an awareness of God's nature which does not appear so fully in the earlier record. Thus we may say of Jehu's massacre of the Baal-worshippers, that he offered it in loyalty to the Lord; the loyalty was good, but the means he used were evil, and so Hosea with a deeper and growing understanding spoke the Lord's condemnation of the bloodshed.

We have seen something of the variety and complexity of the Old Testament witness. When it speaks to us of the God and Father of our Lord Jesus Christ, it is a precious and vital reinforcement of our understanding. In God's care for all people, his ethical demands, dependence on him rather than on armies, the values of compassion and suffering, the understanding of *shālôm*, we are not far from the mind of Christ.

THE TEACHING OF JESUS

'The ethic of Christ is uncompromisingly pacifist' wrote Reinhold Niebuhr (and he was right) in a work designed to show that it was not binding on all Christians. Other interpretations are accommodations of scripture to a predetermined worldly wisdom.

The basic passage is in the Sermon on the Mount (Matt. 5.3–12), and the corresponding passage in the Sermon on the Plain (Luke 6.20–3). At the outset of the Sermon on the Mount come the Beatitudes, that extraordinary transvaluation of human standards, contrasting apparent reality (as the world sees it) with true reality. Here we are confronted with the words 'How blest are the peace-makers; God shall call them his sons' (Matt. 5.9). The Hebrew idiom here is important. To be a 'son of lies' is to be permeated through and through with deceit, what we call a congenital liar. To be a son of God is to be permeated through and through with God. This means that God is a peace-maker. We may link this with two passages in the epistles. Christ 'is our peace' (Eph. 2.14); he makes peace between us. Peace is his gift (John 14.27). If Christ is peace, and whoever has seen Jesus has seen the Father (John 14.9), then God is peace as he is love (1 John 4.9). Then again in the great eighth chapter of Romans, Paul sees the troubles of the present time as the agonies preceding childbirth. What is the birth for which the world is waiting? The glorious freedom of the children of God (Rom. 8.21). Who are the children of God? The peacemakers. It is for the peacemakers that the world is waiting in agony.

Both the Sermon on the Mount and the Sermon on the Plain teach that we are not to be obsessed with security. Both tell us to love our enemies (Matt. 5.44; Lk. 6.28). The Greek word *echthros* embraces both personal and corporate enemies. The context shows that Jesus has in mind, among other things, the attitude of the Jewish people to the Romans; it was the Roman soldiers who might conscribe Jews to carry their packs for a mile (Matt. 5.41). But, in any case, it would have been impossible, literally impossible, for Christ's hearers to make a distinction between the calling of the individual and the community. The Torah was the way of life for the whole people and for the individuals comprising it.

The love here enjoined towards enemies is part of the total teaching of Jesus. 'To love God and to love our neighbour – on these two commandments hang all the law and the prophets' (Matt. 22.37–40). Love is the stamp, the hallmark, of the new community (John 15.12). This love is not an ideal way for an ideal world. It is laid upon Christ's weak and sinful followers in a violent and sinful world. We are not called to turn the other cheek only in the world in which no one strikes us on the first cheek! It is not an ethic offered for the brief period till the expected Second Coming. It is rooted in the nature and being of God, who sends sun and rain upon just and unjust alike; we are to love in order to be children of our Father in heaven.

The characteristic forms of love are compassion and forgiveness and the characteristic fruits, helping and healing. To love does not depend on merit in the one loved or response on their part. God's love is shown in that Christ died for us while we are still sinners (Rom. 5.8). Love involves means as well as ends. There are difficult words in the Sermon on the Mount, rendered in the older versions 'Resist not evil' (Matt. 5.39). It is uncertain exactly what this means, though almost any possible interpretation points to pacifism. But the teaching of Paul in Romans 12 shows what he inherited from the first Christians as the Lord's teaching. Here it is: 'Never pay back evil for evil. . . . Do not let evil conquer you, but use good to defeat evil' (Rom. 12.17–21). This is based on Christ's words, perhaps on some similar occasion, and is, in fact, an earlier record of his teaching. It does not sentimentally pretend that evil does not exist. It means that we are not to meet it with its own weapons, evil with evil, violence with violence.

The conclusion is also unsentimental. There is no promise that the man who hits you on the first cheek will not hit out when you present the other. We are to go on forgiving offences not seven times, but indefinitely. It is true that some notable experiments by P.A. Sorokin with violent individuals showed that if they were treated with violence, it was three to one that their violence would intensify; if with love, that is with constructive and positive approaches, three to one that they would respond constructively and positively. Those are not bad odds, humanly speaking: fifteen to one in favour of love. But Jesus insists that in the sixteenth case it is still right. He does not promise cheap success. He does not say that if the Jews will only make friends with the Romans, everything will be all right; he was not of the collaborating Sadducee party any more than he was of the Zealot freedom fighters. (He does say that if the Jews pursue the way of violence, they will be annihilated.) He promises his followers persecution and hardship. It is still right because it is God's way and God will use such obedience beyond human calculation to bring his transforming power of redemption and liberation.

THE HISTORICAL CONTEXT

Judea was occupied by the Roman military power and the Jews were awaiting a Liberator, the Messiah. (It is important to see that the word 'Saviour' has acquired overtones not in the original, which can mean healer, victor, or liberator.) Clearly, some thought Jesus might be he. 'We have found the Messiah' (John 1.41). 'We had been hoping that he was the man to liberate Israel' (Luke 24.21). Some of his closest followers may have come in that expectation, Simon the Zealot (though it may mean only 'enthusiast'), Simon *bariona* (perhaps 'Son of John', but an Aramaic word for a freedom fighter), James and John ('Sons of Thunder', who wanted to destroy a hostile village), Judas Iscariot (possibly *sicarius*, dagger-man). None of this is certain, though it is plausible that such should seek to be close to him; they would be surprised to find Matthew, a collaborator.

There are some key episodes in the life of Jesus. The first is the Temptations, which included the temptation to secure the kingdoms of this world on terms not God's. In context, this means by military power.

In Luke, the next recorded episode is the sermon in Nazareth (Luke 4.16–30); some have called it the Nazareth manifesto. Jesus reads from Isaiah 61, stopping in mid-sentence so that he does not read 'a day of vengeance for our God' and putting in a verse from Isaiah 58 about deliverance from oppression. The Nazareth manifesto is good news to the poor, release for prisoners (mostly prisoners of war: prison was not used for punishment), healing for the blind, deliverance for the oppressed, and God's Year of Jubilee, when the resources of the land were equitably redistributed. In his presence, all this is true. He goes on to make clear that it applies not just to the Jews, but to all peoples.

The one miracle which appears in all four gospels is the Feeding of the Five Thousand. The people are flocking to Jesus. He takes a boat to get away from them. They come round the shore. He has pity on them 'because they are as sheep without a shepherd' (Matt. 9.36). This was a stock Zealot phrase for the people awaiting their resistance leader. He taught them. What? Presumably, nothing very different from the Sermon on the Mount and the Sermon on the Plain – love of enemies. Then, he organised them into military companies of 50 or 100. Surely the revolution was beginning! It was, but not as they expected. He gave them the Messianic banquet of shared life and dismissed them. John, the most politically alert of the gospel writers, tells how they tried to crown him King, but he withdrew to the hills by himself (John 6.15).

At Caesarea Philippi, Jesus asked the disciples what people were saying about him. Peter said that he was the Messiah. Jesus went on to say that the Son of Man must suffer. Peter protested, and Jesus said 'Away with you, Satan' (Matt. 16.23; Mark 8.33). Peter was renewing the temptation in the wilderness. Jesus then spoke of his followers 'taking up the cross' (Matt. 16.24; Mark 8.34; Luke 9.23). He knew that he was going to be crucified. Crucifixion was a Roman penalty for revolutionary activity, not a Jewish penalty for blasphemy. We may not say that Jesus was politically quietist. He was executed for being a revolutionary and knew that this would happen. Martin Hengel has called him a 'non-violent revolutionist'.

When Jesus entered Jerusalem he was faced with two strands of prophecy. In one, the Messiah would gird his sword upon his thigh and ride out on a white charger as a warrior-king (Ps. Sol. 17–18; 4 Ezra). In the other, the Messiah would come humbly upon a donkey, to put an end to weapons of war and bring peace to non-Jews as well as Jews all the world over (Zech. 9.9–10). He chose the latter, offering the way of peace. When he came in sight of the city he wept, precisely because they did not know the way of peace. He foresaw that they would choose war and meet destruction (Luke 19.41–4). Jesus wanted the whole Jewish people to take the path of non-violence. His pacifism was not merely for isolated individuals, but for the nation.

In Gethsemane he faced arrest. Peter drew a sword to defend him. Jesus said, 'Put up your sword. All who take the sword die by the sword' (Matt. 26.51–2). Jesus could at this point have raised the standard of violent revolt; he did not. He went to the cross. His words condemn all violence. They were not spoken to an aggressor, a Hitler or a gangster. They were spoken to a loyal follower who misguidedly sought to use violence to defend an innocent man from wrongful violence. They are the clearest possible condemnation of all wars, however 'defensive' or 'just'. Tertullian said that in these words the Lord disarmed every soldier.

So he went to the cross. They released a freedom fighter, and he was crucified between two freedom fighters. Hebrews says, 'It was clearly fitting that God for whom and through whom all things exist should, in bringing many sons to glory, make the Captain of their liberation perfect through sufferings' (2.10). The military metaphor is right; it alludes to the military liberator; but God's liberator acts through suffering violence, not inflicting it. Paul notes that the Cross is a stumbling-block. It is seen as folly and weakness (1 Cor. 1.23). To those who follow worldly wisdom and assert the need for 'strength', this is still true. 'But the folly of God is wiser than human wisdom and the weakness of God is stronger than human strength' (1 Cor. 1.25). By God's power, not by human calculations, Good Friday becomes Easter. By God's power, not by human calculations, the way of non-violent love can still transform our human situations.

There is thus a consistent strand running through the gospel narratives relating to the political context of Roman military oppression. The way of Christ is not freedom fighting, escapism, quietism or collaboration. It is an independent way, the way of non-violent suffering love. It is explicitly laid on all who would follow him.

THE INDWELLING CHRIST

In the deepest sense, the Christian life is not an attempt to follow Christ's precepts (for love is not law), nor the imitation of Christ (though that, too, is a precious thought), but, in Paul's words, 'Christ in you, the hope of glory' (Col. 1.27). So he says, 'I live, yet not I; Christ lives in me (Gal. 2.20). We may properly link this to the promise of the Holy Spirit (John 14.16; 16.13, etc.). The Spirit is sometimes called the Spirit of God (Rom. 8.14) or the Spirit of Christ (Rom. 8.9). He is at all times with those who open their lives to him.

What this means is that we have to ask the question, not 'What does God want me to do?', but 'What will Christ do in me?' The Christ we meet in the New Testament will not meet Roman, Russian or American aggression with nuclear weapons, endangering the very creation. He will not meet political tyranny with the bombs which were dropped on Coventry or Dresden. He will not confront evil men with a bayonet, a gun, or a crossbow. To be of Christ is to say 'No' to war in any form, and 'Yes' to peace in its fullest sense and to non-violent love, no matter where that leads us and others.

SOME DIFFICULTIES ANSWERED

Some people have picked on isolated passages which might seem on a casual reading to point in a different direction. This is not really so, but it is proper to examine these passages with especial care. However, before we begin on these, it is as well to clear away one common misapprehension. It is sometimes said that because we are members of society, we cannot escape from the corporate sin of violence and, therefore (it is implied), should not stand aside from a particular manifestation of it. It cannot be too strongly said that Christ was in the same condition – involved in the corporate life, 'yet without sinning' (Heb. 4.15).

In the passage concerning the Cleansing of the Temple, it must be clear that the El Greco image of Christ thrashing the money-changers with a flailing whip is unscriptural. That he was flamingly angry is clear enough: anger is one of the sinews of the soul, and we are too scared of it. The story is told in all four gospels (Matt. 21.12,13; Mark 11.15–17; Luke 19.45–6; John 2.14–16). Only John mentions a whip and expressly says that it was a whip of small cords (useless for aggression), and that he used it to shepherd out the animals (John 2.15). There is nothing here, literally nothing, to justify war. (S.G.F. Brandon's view that the story covers up a major military takeover of part of the Temple is pure fantasy.)

In Matthew 10.34–5, Jesus says that he has 'not come to bring peace, but a sword'. That this is metaphorical is shown in the corresponding passage of Luke (12.51), where in place of 'sword', we have 'division'. We must also note the Semitic idiom; Jesus is speaking of the *result*, not the *purpose*, of his coming.

In Luke 22.36–8, Jesus says that if anyone has no sword he should sell his cloak to buy one. The disciples show him two swords and he replies, 'Enough, enough!' This is on the face of it the most difficult passage. However, there is wide agreement among theologians not known for their pacifism that the words cannot be taken literally. So J.M. Creed: 'It is unlikely that Jesus seriously entertained the thought of armed resistance, which indeed would be in conflict with the whole tenor of his life and teaching.' F.C. Burkitt: 'It is impossible to believe that the command to buy a sword was meant literally or seriously.' It is rather, as William Barclay says, 'a vivid eastern way of telling the disciples that their very lives are at stake'. Jesus' reply is not suggesting that two swords are adequate to face the power of Rome; it is an exclamation of impatience at the disciples' obtuseness. It indicates, says George Caird, 'not satisfaction with the disciples' military preparedness, but a sad dismissal of the subject'. It should be added that the possession of swords at this point and in Gethsemane has nothing to do with military preparedness; it was normal to carry a sword as protection against wild animals.

It is sometimes said that Jesus did not seek to turn Roman soldiers from their profession. In fact, we have no certain record of an encounter with Roman soldiers, except after his arrest. In Luke's version of the healing of the centurion's servant (Luke 7.2–10), the centurion sends a message. Certainly Jesus commends his faith, but that does not imply approval of his profession; he commends the faith of a prostitute, a super-intendent of taxes and, no doubt, numerous slave-owners.

'Pay Caesar what is due to Caesar, and pay God what is due to God' (Mark 12.17). It is doubtful how much we should build on this ingenious answer to a trick question. We should,

however, remember that Caesar does not represent consti-
tutional democratic authority, but alien totalitarian rule. On
the face of it, the words imply that citizens must not accord to
the political authorities the things which are due to God, which
include the ethical quality of our actions.

In Romans 13, Paul says that the authorities do not hold the
power of the sword for nothing. This has been taken to justify
war. In context, it refers simply to the maintenance of law and
order and the punishment of offenders. Christians are not
anarchists (cf. 1 Peter 2.13–17); an ordered society is God's will
for the world. Paul is writing to the Christians in Rome, many of
whom will have been Jewish, and is warning them not to rise in
armed revolt, as the Jews in Palestine did in AD 66. The chapter
divisions are modern: the thirteenth chapter must be read in the
context of the unequivocal pacifism which ends the twelfth.
C.H. Dodd put it well: 'The Christian takes no part in the
administration of a retributive system; but, in so far as it serves
moral ends, he must submit to it. He himself lives by a higher
principle, and he obeys the Government, not because he fears
the retribution which follows on disobedience, but because his
conscience bids him to do so.'

As to the apocalyptic warfare as seen or foreseen in Revelation, these are spiritual battles. Windisch wrote, as long ago as
1909: 'Heavenly beings and superhuman heavenly powers alone
wage war on God's behalf. When men fight, they are doomed to
destruction; only the devil lets men fight for him. The fighters
whom God blesses cannot be men.' In the last chapter of
Ephesians, we are given the weapons of the Christian: truth for a
belt, integrity for a coat of mail, the gospel of peace for footwear,
faith for a shield, salvation for a helmet, and God's words for a
sword (Eph. 6.10–17).

WHAT IS AT STAKE

What is at stake here is our understanding of the Christian
faith. Do we believe in the power of God? Non-pacifists often say
that we have to go to war because the only alternative is to allow
tyranny to win. In the end, that is atheism. To believe in God is
to believe that if we follow his way, no matter what darkness we
pass through, the victory is his.

Do we believe in the Incarnation? Non-pacifists often say that
it is impossible in a human life to follow God's way: we have to

calculate 'the lesser of two evils' (they do not explain how you weigh tyranny against war). This is to deny the Incarnation; it is to say either Christ was not fully human or he did not follow God's way.

Do we believe in the authority of Christ's teaching? Non-pacifists often say, 'Ah, but it wouldn't work.' Christ's teaching is to love our enemies, not to cast out Satan by Satan, not to meet evil with evil, but to overcome it with good, to take not the sword, but the Cross. Are we to throw this overboard?

Do we believe in the Cross? God, faced with the evil in the world, reached out with an unending love and when that failed to win it, could only suffer. This is the way by which God overcomes evil in this world. He lays this way upon all followers of Christ.

Do we believe in the Church as the Body of Christ? If so, our unity with our fellow Christians in Poland, Hungary, Russia and Argentina is greater than our unity with those who are our fellow citizens by accident of birth or geography. We cannot allow the unity of the body of Christ to be broken by governments.

Do we believe in the indwelling Christ? Could he, in any circumstances, drop a nuclear bomb – or stick a sword or bayonet into an enemy? If not, he cannot do so in us.

CONCLUSION

There is a wise and wonderful saying of A.J. Muste: 'There is no way to peace. Peace is the way.' Christ is the Way. Christ is our peace.

The Orthodoxy of Pacifism
Clive Barrett

IT is sometimes claimed that pacifism is a vocation, an option for a chosen few, rather like monasticism. A handful of people are permitted to witness to the somewhat uncomfortable gospel values of love of enemy and peacemaking, whilst everyone else gets on with the more respectable task of preparing to kill each other in warfare.

For Christians to claim that pacifism is but one option of several is for them to misunderstand both the gospel and Christian tradition. Far from being the vocation of a minority, pacifism was a hallmark of orthodox Christianity for over 200 years. This was not just because of the idolatry in the Roman army. It was specifically because one could not take up arms and kill an enemy and still be a Christian.

The early Church Fathers were converted to a Christianity which had yet to be polluted by centuries of worldly power (following the conversion of Constantine in 312). They are best qualified to interpret the mind of the New Testament. The Church today takes great notice of the early Christians' interpretation of doctrine. We should also listen to their ethical arguments. Their words lead to the unambiguous conclusion that pacifism is the only acceptable position for orthodox Christians. Pacifism is not an option for a few, it is mainstream Christianity.

JUSTIN MARTYR (writing c.138):

> You can be convinced that this happened . . . We who used to kill one another, do not make war on our enemies. We refuse to tell lies or deceive our inquisitors: we prefer to die acknowledging Christ.

We who were filled with war and mutual slaughter and all wickedness, have each and all throughout the earth changed our instruments of war, our swords into ploughshares, and our spears into farming tools, and cultivate piety, justice, love of humankind, faith and the hope which we have from the Father, through the Crucified One.

IRENAEUS (c.130–c.200) describes Christians as peoples who 'have made their warlike lances and swords into ploughs and changed them into sickles which he gave for reaping corn, and now do not know how to fight, but when struck offer even the other cheek.'

CLEMENT OF ALEXANDRIA (c.150–c.215): 'We Christians are a peaceful race . . . bred not for war but for peace.'

In a passage appealing for equal treatment for women: 'We do not train women like Amazons to be manly in war, since we wish even men to be peaceable.'

TERTULLIAN (c.160–c.225): 'The Lord's capacity for suffering was wounded in Malchus, and so he cursed the works of the sword for ever.'

'Christ, in disarming Peter, ungirt every soldier.'

There is evidence that from 170/180 a few individuals tried to combine being soldiers and being Christian. Tertullian rejects this way absolutely, upholding the pacifist position always assumed by the Church. He asks in amazement:

'Shall the Son of Peace, for whom it is unlawful to go to law, be engaged in battle?'

'How will a Christian take part in war, nay, how will he serve even in peace?'

'If we are enjoined to love our enemies, whom have we to hate? If injured we are forbidden to retaliate. Who can suffer injury at our hands?'

ORIGEN (c.185–254): 'No longer do we take the sword against any nation, nor do we learn war any more, since we have become sons of peace through Jesus who is our author.'

Jesus 'taught that it was never right for his disciples to go so far [the taking of human life] against a man, even if he should be very wicked.'

'It was impossible for Christians to follow Mosaic law in killing their enemies.'

With Origen we have some of the clearest evidence for the orthodoxy of Christian pacifism. He had to face severe criticism from pagans of the Christian tradition of refusing military service. He acknowledges and affirms the tradition by replying simply: 'We defend the empire in a better way.'

CYPRIAN (d.258): 'God has willed that iron be used for tilling the earth; therefore he has forbidden its use for taking human life.'

'The hand that has held the Eucharist must not be stained with blood and the sword.'

He denounces war: 'Murder, which in the case of an individual is admitted to be a crime, is called a virtue when it is committed wholesale.'

LACTANTIUS (c.240–c.320):

> It will not be lawful for a just man to engage in warfare . . . It is the act of putting to death itself which is prohibited. Therefore, with regard to this precept of God, there ought to be no exception at all, but that it is always unlawful to kill a man, whom God willed to be a saved creature.
>
> How can a man be just who hates, who despoils, who puts to death? And they who strive to be serviceable to their country do all these things.

He condemns any form of retaliation – the sort of motive upon which modern policies of deterrence are based: 'For he who endeavours to return an injury, desires to imitate that very person by whom he has been injured. Thus he who imitates a bad man can by no means be good.'

At the end of the third century, a number of soldiers were put on trial for laying down their weapons when they were converted to Christianity.

MAXIMILIAN (martyred, 295): 'I cannot be a soldier. I cannot do evil. I am a Christian.'

TARACHUS: 'Because I was a Christian, I have now chosen to be a civilian.'

MARCELLUS (martyred, 298): 'I have thrown them [his weapons] away, for it is not fitting that a Christian who fights for Christ his Lord should be a soldier according to the brutalities of this world.'

There are various examples of the Christian language of spiritual warfare being contrasted with the physical warfare which is unacceptable to Christians.

One of the most famous soldier-converts lived in the following century.

MARTIN (316–97) also left the army after being converted: 'I am a soldier of Christ: it is not lawful for me to fight.'

He rejects accusations of cowardice: 'I will take my stand unarmed before the line of battle tomorrow, and in the name of the Lord Jesus, protected by the sign of the cross and not by shield or helmet.'

VITRICIUS, a priest and another former soldier, was told by Paulinus of Nola (353/4–431): 'You have thrown away the arms of blood and, as it were, put on the arms of peace. You have scorned to be armed with the sword because you were armed with Christ.'

Soon, only clergy were entitled to avoid military service. Yet even in the age of Constantine there is still evidence of many people trying to follow the gospel. Fourth-century legal texts on the behaviour of catechumens are good examples:

APOSTOLIC TRADITION: 'The catechumen or believer who wishes to become a soldier will be dismissed because this is far from God.'

TESTAMENT OF OUR LORD: 'If soldiers wish to be baptised in the Lord, let them cease from military service.' Even when Christians were permitted to be in the army, it was only to do police work. If there was war, they had to leave. They were not to kill.

With the conversion of Constantine and the establishment of Christianity, the values of Christianity were reduced to those of the world. As JEROME (c.342–420) said, 'As the Church increased in influence, it decreased in Christian virtues.'

Following Cicero, AMBROSE (c.339–97) and then AUGUSTINE (354–430) developed the concept of a just war (in order to justify war). Before the end of the fourth century, the Roman army was 100 per cent Christian. The orthodoxy of Christian pacifism had been largely forgotten.

Pacifism has been reclaimed by mainstream churches in the twentieth century beginning with the foundation of the FOR in 1964, and the Quakers constant witness to pacifism from the 17th Century. The Anglican Pacifist Fellowship has been part of this movement. Inspired by Dick Sheppard, with the Revd R. Gofton-Salmond, Paul Gliddon, Gilbert Shaw, R.H. Le Messurier and Ursula Roberts among its founders on 11 June 1937. Members have included Percy Hartill, Evelyn Underhill, George Lansbury, Maude Roydon, Vera Brittain, Charles Raven, Gertrude Fiswick (who 'triggered off the chain reaction which ended in CND'), Canon Collins and many other influential figures in the modern peace movement.

For national leaders, new weapons have failed to bring a new consciousness. Yet for many previously uncertain of the merits of pacifist arguments, the ever increasing horror of the weaponry of the nuclear age means that pacifism (in the sense of opposition to war) is the only path available for today's Christians.

The New Covenant
and the Kingdom of God
Gordon Wilson

WHY is violence regarded by pacifists as the worst of evils? Surely, it is often argued, violence is frequently used as a last resort to achieve good ends, serving the true purpose of Christ. The reason why pacifists are so adamant in their rejection of violence is because its use is contradictory to the way of love, which for Jesus is the supreme good. Violence strikes at the very heart of the Christian gospel. Central to this gospel is the New Covenant, which is the distinctive feature of Christianity, as the Old Covenant was the distinctive feature of the religion of the Jews.

The New Covenant was clearly of supreme importance to Jesus and was intended to be so for his followers. It was inaugurated (together with a New Commandment [John 13.34] to which his followers were to be absolutely committed) on the very eve of his own act of absolute commitment to the way of love and was sealed by his own sacrificial blood, symbolised at the Supper by the shared wine: 'This is my blood of the New Covenant' (Luke 22.20). The prophecy of Jeremiah was fulfilled:

> This is the covenant I will make with the house of Israel when those days arrive – it is the Lord who speaks. Deep within them I will plant my Law, writing it on their hearts. Then I will be their God and they shall be my people. There will be no further need for neighbour to try to teach neighbour, or brother to say to brother, 'Learn to know the Lord!' No, they will all know me, the least no less than the greatest – it is the Lord who speaks – since I will forgive their iniquity and never call their sin to mind.
>
> (Jer. 31.33–34)

Without the New Covenant, the teaching of Jesus does indeed represent an unattainable ideal. The New Covenant enables the humblest follower of Jesus to put the teaching into practice. It is the means, and so it was intended, by which the New Age of Christ is inaugurated.

The argument about whether Christians should be pacifists revolves around the question of whether the ideal represented by the Sermon on the Mount is attainable or not. All will recognise without too much difficulty that the Sermon on the Mount, with its injunction to 'turn the other cheek' (Matt. 5.39) and to love one's enemies, presents a pacifist ideal. What people cannot agree upon is whether this ideal is to be put into practice here and now, in the harsh world as it is. That is because, even in the Church, there is still a failure to grasp the significance of the New Covenant as a solemn commitment to follow Jesus on the way of the Cross and to put the New Commandment of love into effect immediately.

The New Covenant is a compact of love, like the marriage covenant, with a lifelong commitment. The Old Covenant was a contract to obey a code of rules. The followers of Christ have freely entered into a compact as equal partners who undertake the same commitment as Jesus himself made and are willing to take the same way that he took – again, like lovers in a marriage rather than servants obeying a master. Love cannot be subject to a code of rules; but the demands of love are limitless, and so are the sacrifices which have to be made in its service. True love demands that the partners in a covenant of marriage are faithful to their commitment, no matter what the circumstances, for as long as they live. The true love offered and demanded by Christ in the New Covenant requires a faithfulness as complete as this. Just as forceful coercion is unthinkable within a loving marriage relationship, so the recourse to forceful coercion represents a failure of commitment within the compact of love which Jesus called the New Covenant. That is why forceful coercion or violence is anathema to those committed to the way of the New Covenant; and this is why the use of violence is regarded by pacifists as the supreme evil, because it is a betrayal of the compact of love.

The way of the Cross is the way of acceptance of the consequences of love and a refusal to respond to injury by violence. It is the way of pacifism. But it is a mistake to assume that to take the way of the Cross and of pacifism represents a mere passive acceptance of evil and its consequences. All Christians believe and speak of the way of the Cross as the way of victory. Pacifists believe that it is literally the *only* way of victory and that the use of violence actually prevents victory in the long run, whatever it may seem to achieve in the short run. Therefore pacifism is a positive faith and not at all the negative avoidance of confrontation which it is usually accused of being. For, although the Cross seemed to represent total, even abject, defeat, it was followed by the Resurrection. The faith of pacifists, as of all Christians, is based ultimately on the Resurrection – a Resurrection which follows total acceptance of the way of the Cross.

The Christian Church knows well enough that this is essentially the gospel it preaches. Why are not all Christians pacifists? It is inexplicable that the Church seems incapable of translating its Easter faith into practical politics in the world, however frequently it recognises in theory that this should be done. How long can this failure continue in the face of the ultimate threat which nuclear violence now poses to all life and all meaning in life? The Lambeth Conference (a gathering of Anglican bishops from all parts of the world which is held every ten years) has long recognised the incompatibility between war and the way of Christ. As long ago as 1930, the Lambeth Conference declared: 'War, as a method of settling international disputes, is incompatible with the teaching and example of our Lord Jesus Christ.' This declaration has been repeated at every Lambeth Conference since 1930. The Lambeth Conference of 1978 added a theological insight to this declaration:

> Jesus, through his death and Resurrection, has already won the victory over all evil. He made evident that self-giving love, obedience to the way of the Cross, is the way to reconciliation in all relationships and conflicts. Therefore the use of violence is ultimately contradictory to the gospel.

There could not be a clearer statement of Christian pacifist belief than that. On the basis of this statement of essential Christian beliefs, with which one could hardly find a single Christian to disagree, one can only assume that for practical purposes most Christians believe that in this 'fallen world' (a phrase which crops up again and again in discussions on this subject, as though there had never been any redemption) there is no alternative but to pursue a policy which is recognised as contradictory to the gospel. If Christians were to resolve this contradiction, they would have to become pacifists. What is it but a failure to understand the New Covenant which prevents this happening?

The apparent absence in the Church of what it really means to be committed to the New Covenant leaves the politicians believing that the Sermon on the Mount offers to them only an impossible ideal and therefore is not to be taken seriously.

A Conservative MP said in a speech in the House of Commons debate on the air attack made in April 1986 by the United States on Libya:

> The Sermon on the Mount undoubtedly set the highest standard of individual behaviour that anyone could require, but it does not apply to those of us in the House who are responsible for the interests of millions of people.

Here is illustrated one of the most common arguments, frequently used by church leaders themselves, for dismissing the teaching of Jesus as 'unrealistic'. A distinction is made (without any authority or justification from Jesus himself) between public and private morality. The Sermon on the Mount, it is implied, is a standard capable of being achieved or at least aspired to only by a few rare saintly individuals. For the mass of ordinary human beings, it is quite out of reach and for them something more 'realistic' (i.e. violent) is required in order to enable them to survive amidst the harsh realities of this cruel world. The MP should understand (and who but the Church can help him to do so – provided the Church itself understands) that the Sermon on the Mount could only apply to those 'who are responsible for the interests of millions of people' on the basis of a commitment to be faithful to the New Covenant. To wait until the millions have made that commitment before making it oneself would be to delay the arrival of the Kingdom of God for ever. The commitment must begin with oneself as the first step towards persuading the millions to do so.

The Church will only help others understand this by first making its own commitment. Only in this way will this 'fallen world' ever have a hope of being transformed. The Kingdom was announced by Christ with the call to 'Repent!' (Matt. 4.17), which literally means to undergo a revolution in ideas. That the standard required, according to the Sermon on the Mount, of those who are committed to the New Covenant (and the revolution demanded by the call to repent) is not merely an individual but a corporate one is symbolised by the response of all who share in the sacrament of the New Covenant, the Eucharist: 'Though we are many, we are one body, because we all share one bread' (1 Cor. 10.17).

The consequence of this revolution is the new order of Christ. 'When anyone is united to Christ, there is a new world; the old order has gone, and a new order has already begun' (2 Cor. 5.17).

> Your world was a world without hope and without God. But now in union with Christ Jesus you who once were far off have been brought near through the shedding of Christ's blood. For he himself is our peace. Gentiles and Jews, he has made the two one, and in his own body of flesh and blood has broken down the enmity which stood like a dividing wall between them; for he annulled the law with its rules and regulations, so as to create out of the two a single new humanity in himself, thereby making peace. This was his purpose, to reconcile the two in a single body to God through the cross, on which he killed the enmity. So he came and proclaimed the good news: peace to you who were far off, and peace to those who were near by. . . .
>
> (Eph. 2.12–18)

The Easter message of hope for a new world, 'in his victory over the grave a new age has dawned, the long reign of sin is ended, a broken world is being renewed', certainly expresses the spirit of the New Testament; but, alas, this is not reflected in the modern Church, which still looks gloomily on a fallen world and sees no hope of its being transformed into the Kingdom of Christ. Instead of the hope of a new humanity expressed by St Paul in the Letter to the Ephesians, the Church evidently clings to the 'peace' through terror, which it believes has been precariously maintained for forty years (despite many very bloody wars and the spread of fearsome terrorism) by the baleful shadow of nuclear weapons. Certainly there is no evident faith in the peace proclaimed by Christ to those who were far off and to those near by. Is this not a betrayal of the gospel? Is it not time to return to the true message of peace proclaimed in the New Testament (and by pacifists today), even if this does mean learning to love our enemies and turning the other cheek. To love one's enemies is not easy, certainly not real enemies in the actual world we live in. Yet Jesus opened up a new dimension of civilised life when he uttered this command as part of his new order of love. To be able to love our enemies is what distinguishes us humans from the animal realm. Animals can exhibit fierce love of their own and show great faithfulness in their protection. But only human beings are capable of loving enemies, and only a very few of us achieve this standard, which is certainly not possible by mere benevolence. Only a solemn commitment to love through the New Covenant can enable us to reach this standard, the standard of divinity. It was to this standard that Jesus called his friends.

The Church officially came to terms with worldly power with the Edict of Milan in 313 AD. Following a vision in a dream on the eve of the Battle of Milvian Bridge which led to his becoming Emperor, Constantine, having been shown the Cross and told, 'In this sign you shall conquer', had the symbol and the motto painted on his soldiers' shields before sending them into battle. The Church Militant (or perhaps the Church Military) was born (and has walked through the corridors of power ever since), the sword replacing the Cross as its effective symbol, except that, as in the case of Constantine, the Cross has been used by Christian armies for centuries as a battle emblem. Army chaplains have administered the Eucharist (the sacrament of the New Covenant) to Christian soldiers wearing the same uniform as themselves before sending them into battle to slaughter Christian soldiers on the opposing side, who have also just received the same sacrament from their own chaplains. Thus has the betrayal of the New Covenant been complete. The kingdoms of this world have been mistaken for the Kingdom of God.

The divergence between Christian standards and worldly standards is brought home especially sharply in wartime, when it is considered a patriotic duty to contradict a vital part of the teaching of Jesus and actually hate one's enemies. In 1915 the Bishop of London, Dr Winnington Ingram, preached a sermon in St Paul's Cathedral in which he exhorted Young England to: 'kill Germans – to kill them not for the sake of killing, but to save the world, to kill the good as well as the bad, to kill the young as well as the old.' To serve the state has been considered to be on a par with serving Christ. To be a soldier of the state, fighting under the battle emblem of the Cross, has been regarded as fighting for Christ and failure to fight has been regarded as a failure of Christian duty.

Occasionally Christians have rebelled against this betrayal, and often they have paid a heavy price for doing so. During the last war, a simple Christian peasant in Austria, Franz Jägerstätter, refused to fight in Hitler's army because he believed it was contrary to his Christian faith to do so. His parish priest tried hard to persuade him that it was his Christian duty to fight to defend his family and nation. When the priest failed, he called in his bishop to use more subtle persuasive eloquence; but he too failed. Eventually, Jägerstätter was brought before a tribunal, who were so frustrated in their attempts to make him deny his Christian conscience that they pronounced him to be 'suffering from religious mania' and condemned him to execution. In England things were different. Like Jägerstätter, I felt moved by my Christian conscience to refuse to fight. I, too, felt the general weight of Christian opinion against me (though I was supported by my parish priest) and I also appeared before a tribunal. Though I was acknowledged as being 'genuine, sincere', I was declared to be 'bordering on religious mania'. There the similarity with Jägerstätter's case ended. Instead of being beheaded like him, I was given unconditional exemption and thus was free to pursue my studies in preparation for ordination (I had not mentioned this to the tribunal lest they should think it a plea for mitigation).

The attitude of the Church has changed significantly over the period of time from Lambeth 1930 to Lambeth 1978 and up to the present day. Christians in general have become increasingly uneasy about the contradiction between the use of violence and the gospel. When Pope John Paul II visited Ireland in 1979 and contemplated the bitter violence of the struggle there within the community, which though under rival labels bears the most fervent allegiance to Christianity, he summed up the true Christian attitude (and, indeed, the pacifist attitude):

> Communities who stand together in their acceptance of Jesus' supreme message of love, expressed in peace and reconciliation, and in their rejection of all violence, constitute an irresistible force to achieve what many regard as impossible and destined to remain so.

If all Christians everywhere would indeed stand together in this way, then things would be achieved which many regard as impossible. The whole Church would find a unity which many of us from different denominations have already experienced in a mutual commitment to peace. Moreover, the Church would quickly become an irresistible moral force to influence events in ways which many politicians could hardly conceive. The power of the Holy Spirit would be manifest in the Church, as it has hardly been since Pentecost.

It is time for all Christians to enter into their true inheritance; and not only Christians. Just as within the Church, divisions caused by old labels like 'Protestant' and 'Catholic' are (except in areas of tribal political warfare like Northern Ireland) losing their former intensity, so divisions between different religions are disappearing as people of different faiths unite in their pursuit of human unity and peace. Much is being learned as the deepest religious insights are shared and recognition grows of a common humanity in a world now seen to be too small to contain the bitter divisions of the past.

Every year, members of all the great faiths of the world join in a Week of Prayer for World Peace centred on United Nations Day, 24 October. This experience has brought great fellowship and happiness in co-operation in pursuit of a goal which all long for and recognise as human destiny. It is extremely rewarding to share the precious gifts of faith with those who understand their value. A deeply felt common recognition of divine power brings illumination to this spiritual fellowship. Though our modern world has brought great new fears, the growth of a sense of world community has brought unprecedented hope to mankind. The time has come to repent. The spiritual revolution is imminent. The Kingdom of God has been announced. All that is now required is our faith.

Praying for Peace
George Appleton

ST Paul writing to the small group of Christians in Philippi, for whom he had a special affection, urged them to 'Have no anxiety about anything, but in everything by prayer and supplication with thanksgiving let your requests be made known to God' (4.6). That would seem to be a text well worth deep study for all who feel a special call to pray for peace.

So, following Paul's advice, we offer our anxieties, our hopes and prayers to God with thanksgiving. Indeed, there is much to be thankful for. I thank God for the revelation of himself, his will and purpose, his universal love, his unlimited forgiveness, his eternal purpose to gather the whole human race into the divine love (John 11.51–2). We should praise him for the assurance that is given us in the Bible that he is always at work, even in the worst of circumstances, to redeem the most dismaying happenings. We can be grateful for the stirring of conscience everywhere about the tragedy and waste of war, and for the many conferences and demonstrations that are taking place, aimed at avoiding war and finding the way to peace. We can thank God for the growth of compassion among the nations, shown through the immediate aid in emergency and disaster situations, and through pattern activities like Christian Aid, Catholic Fund for Overseas Development, Oxfam, Save the Children Fund, War on Want and others.

I do not hesitate to thank God that governments, nations and political parties are sensitive to public opinion, moral pressure and informed protest, especially when a general election is near. I thank him, too, that the religions of the world are beginning to think and work together for human welfare, social justice and world peace, though much more needs to be done in pursuing those three fundamental aims. Few people know that there is now a World Conference of Religions for Peace (WCRP) which has already held four world assemblies. More and more people are taking part in the annual Week of Prayer for World Peace, initiated by APF, which has until recently published its material for prayer in English, but is now planning for it to be published in the main languages of the world, so that people of all faiths may join together to pray in their own way and in their own language. More immediately, Pope John Paul II invited the religious leaders of the world to meet him in Assisi on 4 October 1986, the feast day of St Francis. Francis went on a peace mission to the camp of the Muslim, Saladin, during the Crusades, and has given us one of the best known and most loved prayers, which begins, 'Lord, make us instruments of your peace', and goes on to pray that hatred may be displaced by love, injury by pardon, discord by unity, doubt by faith, and despair by hope. So with thankfulness in our hearts, we can offer our prayers for peace to the Creator and Lover of us all, whose will is justice and peace.

In that spirit, we go on to pray for the tasks that still have to be done. First and foremost, we must pray for the scaling down of fear in the hearts of all people. Mahatma Gandhi urged us,

> Do not fear, he who fears hates; he who hates kills. Break your sword and throw it away and fear will not touch you. I have been delivered from desire and from fear, so that I know the power of God.

Archbishop Michael Ramsey has given us this insight:

> The human race is afraid and its fears are about power – about having it or not having it. Those who have it are frightened that they may be going to lose it. Those who do not have it are frightened of those with it. This is true of groups, classes, nations and races.

Often we may feel powerless to do anything effective for the cause of peace. At such times we may pray:

> O God, whose blessed Son was powerless in the hands of men and was content to be nailed to the cross when those who had brought him there jeered at his inability to save himself, yet did not fail in love towards all who had a hand in his death: Grant that when we have no power, we may exercise the power of love, and pray that thy righteous and loving will be done, as it was by thy blessed Son, revealing thy unfailing love and unlimited forgiveness.

The first words of the Christian era, heard by shepherds in the fields of Bethlehem, were: 'Be not afraid; for behold, I bring you good news of a great joy which will come to all people' (Luke 2.10). Today there are more than 1,000 million Christians in the world, with Christians in almost every country of the world. If they prayed, not just for one special week in the year, but on every day in the year, that people everywhere may lose their fear, what a joy there would be in the other three-quarters of the world population. So we pray that all of us humans may be delivered from fear and so enrolled in God's army of pray-ers and workers for peace.

There is a more wholesome kind of fear, which is common to both parties when war is threatened or actually breaks out, namely the realisation of the immense destructive power in nuclear energy. When the first atomic bomb was dropped on Hiroshima, 60,000 people were killed in a blinding, burning flash and a similar number died from the effects of radiation. Nuclear bombs today are infinitely more powerful. Realistic fear of retaliation has kept rival nations from engaging in nuclear war for over forty years and for that fact we must be thankful, even though it is said that Russia has enough nuclear weapons to kill everyone in the USA ten times over and, similarly, the USA has enough nuclear weapons to do the same to the people of Russia. Our litany for peace must include some such petition as, 'From all overkill, save us and help us we humbly beseech thee, O Lord', and then go on to pray for our raising man's valuation of human life to God's level, thanking him for his love and care for every single human being and for his plan that mankind shall live together as his family, in the kind of world that he has always been working to create.

In the prayer which Pope John Paul II prayed during his visit to Hiroshima, he says that he speaks 'for the multitudes in every country and in every period of history'. We who do not want war and are ready to join in the struggle for peace can pray it with him:

> To you, Creator of nature and humanity, of truth and beauty I pray: Hear my voice, for it is the voice of the victims of all wars and violence among individuals and nations. Hear my voice, for it is the voice of all children who suffer and will suffer when people put their faith in weapons and war.
> Hear my voice when I beg you to instil into the hearts of all human beings the wisdom of peace, the strength of justice and the joy of fellowship.

Hear my voice, for I speak for the multitudes in every country and in every period of history who do not want war and are ready to walk the road of peace.

Hear my voice and grant insight and strength, so that we may always respond to hatred with love, to injustice with total dedication to justice, to need with the sharing of self, to war with peace. O God, hear my voice, and grant unto the world your everlasting peace.

We live today in a society in which violence is rife. The Christian will remember the rebuke of Jesus to Peter when he attempted a one-man rescue in the Garden of Gethsemane and began to strike out right and left with his sword: 'Put your sword back into its place; for all who take the sword will perish by the sword' (Matt. 26.52). This short direct text tells us a great deal about 'the laws of violence': it is continuous, once you start you cannot get away from it; it is reciprocal, others tend to do to you what you do to them; violence is unlimited, it is not possible to say, 'so far and no further', violence simply begets violence, so the good end is defeated by the wrong means. It is also interesting to note that those who use violence always try to justify it.

So we must try to understand the causes of violence and the bitterness of people who feel that a great injustice has been inflicted on them. At the same time, we must try to introduce into situations of tension and violence, something specifically Christian. When I was Anglican Archbishop in Jerusalem, two of my Arab priests told me that they were members of the Palestinian Liberation Organisation (PLO). I felt that I had no right to object to such political association, but I did feel it right to remind them that they were Christ's representatives within the PLO and that they should pray and work for a just and agreed solution.

An example of how this might be done came from a Buddhist Vietnamese monk, the Venerable Htich Hnat Hanh. In one of his poems he wrote:

Promise me, promise me, this day
   while the sun is at its zenith
     even as they strike you down
   with a mountain of hate and violence,
   remember, brother, man is not our enemy.
     Alone again, I'll go on
   with bent head, but knowing
    the immortality of love.

At an inter-faith conference, I asked him to lead a meditation for all attending it. I still have the paper on which he put down these headings:

As we are together, praying for Peace, let us be truly with each other.

Silence

Let us pay attention to our breathing.

Silence

Let us be relaxed in our bodies and our minds.

Silence

Let us be at peace with our bodies and our minds.

Silence

Let us return to ourselves and become wholly ourselves. Let us maintain a half-smile on our faces.

Silence

Let us be aware of the source of being common to us all and to all living things.

Silence

Evoking the presence of the Great Compassion, let us fill our hearts with our own compassion – towards ourselves and towards all living beings.

Silence

Let us pray that all living beings realise that they are all brothers and sisters, all nourished from the same source of life.

Silence

Let us pray that we ourselves cease to be the cause of suffering to each other.

Silence

Let us plead with ourselves to live in a way which will not deprive other living beings of air, water, food, shelter, or the chance to live.

Silence

With humility, with awareness of the existence of life and of the sufferings that are going on around us, let us pray for the establishment of peace in our hearts and on earth.

Amen

The Venerable Htich Hnat Hanh is the head of the Buddhist Peace Mission and has his headquarters in Paris.

His plea that 'man is not our enemy' reminds me of St Paul's words in his Epistle to the Ephesians, when speaking of the whole armour of God: 'For we are not contending against flesh and blood, but against principalities, against the powers, against the world rulers of this present darkness, against the spiritual hosts of wickedness in the heavenly places' (6.12). The enemies we have to fight are hatred, jealousy, greed, untruths, mistaken ideas of God, 'envy, hatred, malice and all uncharitableness' as the 1662 litany put it.

The weapons which go to make up the whole armour of God are the belt of truth, the breastplate of righteousness, the shield of faith, shoes quick to take the message of peace, the helmet of trust in God's protecting love, and the sword of the spirit, which is the word of God, piercing through all confusions and pretences (Eph. 6.13–20). Those are the only weapons we Christians are permitted to use.

I remember reading a short time ago of the wife of a rabbi who, overhearing her husband's prayer that God would wipe out all evil-doers, prayed that all wickedness should vanish from the earth, which seems to me a more godly prayer.

People often wonder how our prayers for peace and other great world issues can affect such situations. Tragic things happen, cruel deeds are done, things seem to have got out of hand, God's hand as well as ours. How can the prayers of individuals, or even congregations, help to cure such tragedies and widespread evil? The first answer that comes into my mind is that our prayers keep such situations tied to God and prevent him being pushed out. The second clue is that most man-made situations arise from wrong attitudes within the minds and spirits of people, so that the struggle is basically a spiritual one. Prayer is a spiritual activity and, therefore, involves us in that spiritual fight.

This is thinking from the human angle. The more important thought is what God in the mystery of his Being and activity will do. When we intercede, we are offering ourselves to him as channels of his love, goodness and inspiration, for those for whom we pray and the situations about which we pray. One of our ancient collects speaks of God as more ready to hear than we to pray, giving more than we desire or deserve, above all that we ask or think. That should encourage us to pray at all times, whether we feel like it or not, when we grieve about the unholy things that happen or inflammatory speeches that are made.

There are times when protests need to be made against what we believe to be wrong policies and cruel actions. But we need to protest without a spirit of enmity, to persuade and plead for what we believe to be right and wise, rather than to denounce angrily. The Buddha taught that 'hatred ceases not by hatred but by love'. Jesus taught us to love everyone, including our enemies, and to pray for those who harm us. His first word from the Cross was a prayer for all who had brought him to that painful death, even making excuse for them, 'for they know not what they do' (Luke 23.34).

Another feature of our international relations is the way in which all the nations spend their national incomes. Stockholm International Peace Research Institute (SIPRI) tells us that the nations of the world spend £250,000 million on defence and armaments, twice as much as on health and half as much again as on education. We are told that if every nation, poor and rich, would reduce what they spend on defence by 5 per cent each year, world hunger and widespread disease could be overcome in 10 years. The savings could then be used to feed the hungry, provide pure drinking water and step up literacy, education and health services, and so work towards the abundant life which is God's will for all. So I pray regularly and urgently that this may be done and that more and more nations will set an example or declare their willingness to do so as soon as all agree.

We need also to pray for our leaders and governments. For nearly 100 years, churchpeople have prayed a prayer first prayed by Bishop Paget, a former Bishop of Oxford:

> Almighty God, from whom all thoughts of truth and peace proceed: Kindle, we pray thee, in the hearts of all men the true love of peace; and guide with thy pure and peaceable wisdom those who take counsel for the nations of the earth; that in tranquillity thy kingdom may go forward, till the earth is filled with the knowledge of thy love; through Jesus Christ our Lord.

Every year, we hold Remembrance Services on the Sunday nearest 11 November, the day on which the First World War ended. I have taken part in such services in war cemeteries in Beirut, Cairo and Jerusalem, and at war memorials in many towns and villages in Australia and Britain, and have prayed this prayer:

> May the memory of two world wars strengthen our efforts for peace!
> May the memory of those who died inspire our service to the living!
> May the memory of past destruction move us to build for the future!
> May the first two world wars be the last two world wars!
> May the first two nuclear bombs be the last two nuclear bombs!

O God of peace,
O Father of souls,
O Builder of the Kingdom of Love.

There is a prayer, composed by a Jain, based on an ancient prayer from India:

Lead me from death to life,
   from falsehood to truth.
Lead me from despair to hope,
   from fear to trust.
Lead me from hate to love,
   from war to peace.
Let peace fill our heart,
   our world, our universe.

Over a million cards with this prayer have been printed in over 30 languages by the Prayer for Peace Movement, and my heart thrills with joy when I hear it prayed in services I attend.

To be dedicated workers for peace we need to have peace in our hearts. So we may pray:

O God of many names
Lover of all nations
We pray for peace
   in our hearts
   in our homes
   in our nation
   in our world
the peace of your will
the peace of our need.

Each of us can pray in our own words, repeating some short sentence, 'Guide our feet into the way of peace', or 'Give peace in our time, O God', or just saying the word Peace, Pax, Shālôm, Salaam, Shanti, and adding to the word in our own language, the appeal to the God of Peace, the Prince of Peace.

At other times, I have used a devotional meditation which is an extension of a 'prayer' or aspiration, used by the Buddha:

Now may every living thing, young or old, weak or strong, living near or far, known or unknown, living or departed or yet unborn, may every living thing be full of bliss.

One can sit with a quiet heart and mind and send out a radiation of love, joy, compassion and peace in turn, beginning with one's home, neighbourhood, country, other countries, the whole world and then to those in the spiritual sphere whom we speak of as 'dead', but who could more truthfully be described as 'risen ones'.

As a Christian, I have tried to use this life-giving radiation of love in a framework of my belief in God in Christ. So I pray:

> May the peace which passes understanding
> possess the minds of people everywhere,
> banishing all anxiety and perplexity,
> watching sentinel over their hearts and minds,
> refusing entrance to every disturbing thought.
> In everything that happens,
> may people know that all things work together for good
> when they love thee and want thy will.
> Give them thine own peace,
> which the world cannot give and cannot take away.
> Let nations live together in peace
> and know the things that belong unto peace.
> And may thy peace in my heart
> go out to all my fellow people –
> to calm their worries and their enmities,
> to let them know that the peace given me
> is available for them also,
> through him who made himself our Peace,
> even Jesus Christ, our Lord.

Let me close with what is to me the decisive imperative in the thinking, practice and praying of all who profess to be Christian peacemakers. It comes from St Paul's second letter to the disciples at Corinth and it needs no paraphrasing or embellishment:

> If anyone is in Christ, he is a new creation; the old has passed away, behold, the new has come. All this is from God, who through Christ reconciled us to himself and gave us the ministry of reconciliation; that is, God was in Christ reconciling the world to himself, not counting their trespasses against them, and entrusting to us the message of reconciliation. So we are ambassadors for Christ, God making his appeal through us.

> (5.17–20a)

2
PACIFISM
AND
CONFLICT

It is easy for comfortable, white, middle-class Europeans to assent to pacifism. But what of the world's oppressed peoples suffering constantly from overt or institutionalised violence? What is the pacifist perspective from other nations?
In this section, we investigate the crucial question of the relationship between pacifism and justice. We look at the troubles in Ireland and progres made within the church structures of the biggest military power on earth. Leading peace campaigners in Britain consider how Britain's nuclear deterrence policy causes injustices and fear. They explore the nature of current campaigns, emphasise tolerance and show why it is a matter of urgency for us all to support the contemporary peace movement.

Peace and Justice
Paul Oestreicher

IF faith, hope and love are part of the real world, then justice and peace are legitimate goals for the human race. It is the psalmist's dream that ultimately justice and peace will embrace, will kiss each other. There will then be a perfect harmony within the whole creation and between creatures and creator. *Shālôm* is one of several possible words for that ultimate vision. We are talking about what Jesus called the Kingdom of God.

It is important to bear in mind that Jesus did not confine the Kingdom to the future. In embryo, perhaps even more than in embryo, it is already present within us and among us. Heaven, then – or at least some significant part of it – is now; so, very obviously, is hell. The war between them may not be confined to this world, may indeed be cosmic, but while we are here, this is the battleground: within us and among us.

The phrase 'justice and peace', thanks largely to the insights of the Second Vatican Council and to subsequent Roman Catholic social teaching, has become something of an ecumenical cliché, a sort of incantation. It was, I think, Pope Paul VI who coined the related concept that 'the new name for peace is development'. And development, for its part, has become shorthand for the creation of economic justice in two-thirds of the world.

That there is an integral and inescapable relationship between peace and justice is true and is important. Many conflicts stem from real or perceived injustice; but not all. Marx believed wrongly that when socialism has been universally achieved – i.e. when there is true economic justice everywhere –

there would no longer be any reason for civil or international strife. The evidence of personal experience and of history suggests that conflict, be it personal or political, does not need an economic trigger. Its roots lie much more deeply in fallen humanity. Alienation (Marx's word for sin) is not solely the product of injustice. Its causes are much more complex. What can be said with much more confidence is that injustice is rooted in sin, in alienation. (This may indeed be something of a chicken-and-egg problem.) I rejoice that it is now taken for granted in many parts of the universal Church that the struggle for justice is essential to Christian discipleship. Even so, many Christians go on denying this. Those whose main preoccupation is the saving of their soul are well on the way to losing it. The gospel does not merely have social implications. It is inherently and essentially social and, therefore, also political. That does not make it less personal, for it is only through relationships – i.e. in a social context – that we become true persons. There is such a relationship of love within the godhead itself.

The struggle for justice, then, is part of what makes us truly human. To frustrate that struggle, to stand in its way, is a denial of love. To stand aside from that struggle is to be dead to the true and ultimate meaning of Holy Communion.

In saying that, I am identifying with the broad stream of contemporary ecumenical theology. However, I feel bound to part with the commonly held, simplistic assumption that the struggle for justice is virtually identical to or even a precondition for making peace. The relationship between justice and peace is complex and dialectical. The two beatitudes 'Blessed are those who hunger and thirst for righteousness' (Matt. 5.6) and 'Blessed are the peacemakers' (Matt. 5.9) are related, but not the same. Indeed, they are often, in the world as we know it, really or apparently incompatible. This tension needs to be faced. Whether it can be resolved must, for the moment, be left open.

Mainstream Christendom has tacitly recognised the dilemma. It has, in practice, given priority to justice. Peace, on the other hand, has been made an ultimate or, at any rate, a more distant goal. That is the basis of the theology of the just war and of the just revolution. It is the basis of contemporary liberation theology. At its heart is the biblical rebuke to those who cry: '"Peace, peace", when there is no peace' (Jer. 6.14). God, this theology says, is at war with injustice, exploitation and oppression. The Lord is not neutral. He is on the side of the hungry, the poor, the imprisoned, the tortured, the rejected of this world. The Church must, therefore, be a partisan Church. It must – contrary to much of its history – break with the powerful and embrace the weak. There is good biblical warrant for that position. Yet this can only be maintained at the price of shelving the whole agonising problem of reconciliation; agonising, because it takes us directly to the Cross. Can peace somehow be a reality, even in the midst of cruelty and horror? Can forgiveness operate when there is no repentance, when wrongs are not put right? That recent South African theological *cri de coeur*, the *Kairos* document, suggests that the answer is no, a 'no' that echoes down through history. It is a profoundly human 'no'.

Yet where has that 'no' led? To Christians turning their conflicts (often against each other) into holy wars, crusades. In the process, a whole strand of the New Testament has got lost: 'If your enemy is hungry, feed him; if he is thirsty, give him drink; for by so doing you will put him to shame. Do not let evil defeat you but overcome evil with goodness' (Rom. 12.20–1). Even more important than these words of St Paul, writing to the Christians in Rome, even more important than the pacifist precepts of the Sermon on the Mount, is the extraordinary prayer of the dying Jesus: 'Father, forgive them; for they know not what they do' (Luke 23.34). The Cross and Christ's prayer on the Cross suggest that a profound kind of peace may yet be possible, even prior to the end of injustice. Might it not be that the declaration of that peace, of a divine, unilateral truce, may be an alternative route to justice? Does not the doctrine of grace suggest that God has unilaterally declared a truce with fallen humanity? How can we respond?

Clearly, not by being indifferent to injustice. Clearly, not by making no real distinction between the oppressed and their oppressors. Clearly, not by shutting our eyes to the evil of the world. God *is* at war with injustice. So must his servants be. But there is no legitimate escape from the paradox that the same God who is engaged in the battle against sin is in solidarity with sinners. And it is important to remember that 'all have sinned and fall short of the glory of God' (Rom. 3.23). The common bond of fallen, yet redeemed, humanity unites the victim with the torturer. In the context of the divine mercy, the Cross is a bridge even between Hitler and his holocaust victims. The spiritual battle is not only the battle to give bread to the hungry, but to win the souls of the rich. In the conflict between Dives and Lazarus (Luke 16.19–31), the issue of justice is not fudged by clever economic casuistry. Dives is guilty, as wealthy western Christians are guilty, as rapacious Brazilian landowners are guilty. Yet Christ goes on suffering, too, in the not-yet-abandoned soul of the unrepentant tycoon or arms merchant. 'Father forgive, for they know not . . .' is a timeless prayer.

Those who share some fragment of the vision of the divine love, those who have been given the grace to share somehow in the redemptive suffering of Christ are, to a greater or lesser degree, set free from the slavery of hatred and fear. Stephen was able to pray for those stoning him to death (Acts 7.60). Sheila Cassidy was able to pray for her Chilean military torturers. Even the unreligious, with no direct experience of God, are capable of compassion for those in the grip of racial hatred. A Marxist friend of mine, of Jewish background, spares no effort, through tireless encounters, to set young neo-fascists free from their irrational hatreds and fears.

It is also important to remember that no battle for justice is a straight struggle between good and evil, light and darkness. However clear the issue, the liberator does not cease to be a sinner, the oppressor does not cease to carry within him or her the divine image, however marred. The war against Hitler ended with the holocaust of Dresden. The anti-apartheid struggle does not exclude bitter feuds to the death of black against black. The 'pure crusade' is a product not of truth, but of propaganda, of psychological warfare. The world of 'goodies and baddies' belongs to the realm of fiction.

Yet, at the end of the day, none of that is an alibi for neutrality, for staying on the side-lines. The God who bids us love our enemies is not on the side-lines, but in the struggle. There *are* real enemies. There is a kind of wet Christianity which denies the demonic: a misunderstood faith based on the liberal myth that real evil does not exist. When the Temple guards came to arrest Jesus, he was under no illusion that he had fallen into enemy hands. The question his arrest posed was: how does one deal with the enemy? The followers of Jesus were prepared to use their swords to defend him and were rebuked for it (Matt. 26.52). Challenged to summon legions of avenging angels to intervene, he did nothing (Matt. 4.6–7; Luke 4.9–12). But then, it has been argued, Jesus was a special case. It is an unconvincing argument. For he, surely, was the prototype of true humanity. Again, it has been argued: self-defence is not a Christian obligation, the defence of others who are weak and helpless is. Yet Jesus was knowingly not simply sacrificing himself but – as he made quite clear – putting at risk all those he loved: his mother, his disciples, his Church. His fate, he predicted, would and, indeed, should also be theirs. And so, to a large extent, it was, at least until the Emperor himself became a Christian.

The struggle for justice poses no serious ethical problem unless and until it demands action against the unjust which cannot be reconciled with love. Violence is not in itself the problem. Coercive action need not be incompatible with genuine concern for the person against whom it is taken. To forcibly restrain a child from running across a busy road, and even to beat that child if it does, is intended to benefit that child. A police force, even an armed police force, exists – at least ideally – to protect all people. Its purpose is not to destroy even the enemies of society, but to restrain them.

War is inherently different, be it civil or international, guerrilla or legitimate, local or global. It demands the destruction of the enemy, whether narrowly or widely defined. Its purpose is invariably perceived to be the righting of a wrong, the pursuit of justice and, in the end, the restoration of peace. On one current definition, it is the injustice itself that has broken the peace. The just war, therefore, is – paradoxically – fought to restore peace. Ideally, the existence of military power will suffice to deter the evil-doer. Thus, the soldier becomes the peace-keeper. In the past, this ideal has almost invariably broken down. Among nuclear powers today, human survival depends on it not breaking down, either by accident or design; a crazy gamble, given the fallibility of technology and of human nature.

It should be clear from all I have said that the relentless pursuit of human justice makes conflict inevitable. Christians have no mandate to withdraw from the conflict. The question then becomes: are there ways of conducting the conflict which are compatible with genuine love for all those involved in it?

The doctrine of the just (justifiable is what is really meant) war recognises the problem. It abandons the more popular (even today, as evidenced by the public reaction to the Falklands War) idea of the holy war or crusade which must be won for God's sake, regardless of the cost and the means, and puts in its place the concept of war as a necessary or lesser evil. Such a war is – at least in theory – hedged about with restraints. The humanity of the enemy is acknowledged; his wife and children are not legitimate victims, nor even the trees in his garden. This much and more had, long before the time of Jesus, become part of the morality of the people of Israel. The doctrine of the just war is an Old Testament ethic, reinstated and elaborated by Christian theologians from Augustine (354–430) onwards. The prophets of Israel began to know God as a God of peace who took no pleasure in war.

But the Church, since the third century, has really been split: some Christians have always resolutely said 'no' to armed conflict and have occasionally been martyred for it; some have opted for so-called realism, reluctantly saying 'yes' to war for the sake of some greater good, but war with considerable restraints – the prevailing just war orthodoxy – and yet in practice, the wars of Christian history have usually ended up as crusades. The memorials in the cathedrals of Christendom testify to it. To die in battle has long been regarded as a more or less direct ticket to heaven. The 'supreme sacrifice' was readily identified with Calvary. It is all there in the almost pagan theology of that powerfully emotive hymn, 'O Valiant Hearts'.

In a revolutionary context, the same romance surrounds the death of the Marxist, Che Guevara, and the Christian, Camillo Torres. There is, who can deny it, a real kind of nobility in blood spilt for a good cause; the blood makes the cause sacred. And yet, at the heart of this kind of 'martyrdom' there is at least a double contradiction. Both sides, often invoking the same God, believe their cause to be sacred. The First World War is a good case in point. And then, when the memorials are erected, it has to be forgotten that every good soldier is taught to kill and, if at all possible, to survive. That, too, is every good freedom fighter's duty.

Where does that leave the pacifist who refuses to kill? Is he not indeed crying, ' "Peace, peace," when there is no peace' (Jer. 6.14)? Is he not opting out of the struggle for justice, when all peaceful means of change have failed? Or is he simply making an important minority witness, of no immediate political relevance, to the ultimate values of the Kingdom, while the main body of Christendom struggles with the morally more ambiguous realities of the penultimate? Was the young Rhodesian Methodist not profoundly right, during the freedom struggle of his people, when he said to me: 'Until we are free, I must suspend my Christianity and fight.' He saw the contradiction, as Dietrich Bonhoeffer did when he joined the plot to kill Hitler. He imbued that with no heroic romance: 'I must do what I must do and can then only ask to be forgiven.' That commands respect. But it cannot be the final answer. Perhaps there is no such answer. Perhaps there is. Perhaps we are not all called to the same kind of discipleship. That makes sense if obedience to conscience, to the Inner Light, must, for each of us in this world, be the last word. The soldier and the conscientious objector are then, at the same time, witnessing to complementary but – at a given moment in history – incompatible truths.

But I am far from sure whether Christian discipleship permits and enshrines that degree of subjective judgment. As I struggled with the gospel's radical vision of justice, on the one hand, radical because absolute love embraces but goes far beyond justice, and the gospel's even more radical vision of a peace from which no fragment of creation is excluded, Mahatma Gandhi came to my rescue. Why should not this spirit-filled Hindu politician and mystic be in a position to help Christians come to a deeper understanding of the mind of Christ? I have certainly been so helped.

It was Gandhi's conviction that to recognise evil and not to oppose it was to deny one's humanity. To recognise evil and to oppose it with the weapons of the evil-doer was to affirm one's humanity. To recognise evil and to oppose it with the weapons of God was to affirm one's divinity.

Here is a holy Hindu recognising that human beings are capable of being less than human, of being human and of being more than human. Does that not reflect our real experience? Not to care at all is a familiar form of depravity. We recognise it in ourselves and in others. The results are demonic. If even a significant minority of Germans had cared about the fate of the Jews, the holocaust would not have happened. The Church has no alibi.

Of most help to me, the Christian pacifist, is Gandhi's 'middle axiom': in effect he, the apostle of non-violence, says to fight evil with the weapons of the evil-doer (i.e. to go to war) is better than not to fight at all. It is the human thing to do. Here, from Gandhi, is an apologia for the just war. Here is the great mystic expressing real understanding of the way of the world at its human best. Here is the real ground for the pacifist to respect the soldier and the freedom fighter. The peace campaigner who implicitly or explicitly simply equates war with murder reveals himself to be something of a self-righteous bigot. (Though war often comes close to being just that!) To leave this legitimate opening for war is to leave a comparable opening for what some will call terrorism. One man's freedom fighter is – as we know – another man's terrorist.

Most human beings and most Christians with them have, until now, expressed their humanity through Gandhi's middle way, as the best or only possible option. Jesus, Gandhi, Martin Luther King and others with them suggest that a third way is possible, that human beings are capable of transcending their humanity and entering into their divinity. What is suggested here – a doctrinal idea worthy of exploration – is that we are enabled to share in both natures of Christ, the human and the divine. In Christian mysticism, that is nothing new. It must now be translated into practical forms of Christian realism. What I am talking about are strategies for defeating evil with goodness. It is at this point that the Christian soldier and freedom fighter is called to listen to and learn from the pacifist for both practical and spiritual reasons.

Might it not be that the development of weapons technology is now bringing the human family rapidly to the point at which violent means will no longer be usable to achieve good ends? Might it not be that in the third millennium of the Christian era, weapons will have to become obsolete if the human race is to survive? Might it not be that only the pacifist who refuses to use lethal weapons is tomorrow's realist? But war or no war, the struggle for justice will need to go on. It may become true sooner than I have suggested that peace, meaning the absence of armed conflict, is a precondition for justice and not, as many still believe, the other way round. It evidently takes a long time for the Holy Spirit to lead the human family – and the Church – into all truth. Perhaps we shall learn, sooner than even most pacifists dare to hope, that it is possible – by the grace of God – to overcome evil with costly, self-sacrificing love. There is a crossroads ahead: the options are destruction or survival. Might it now be the Church's task to show that the age of blood sacrifice must end? Or might it be the world that teaches this to an increasingly irrelevant Church? One way or another, such a miracle is surely not too much to ask for.

Christian Peacemaking: Lessons from Ireland

David Bleakley

I write as one who has laboured in the vineyard of peace in Ireland for many years. It has been an illuminating experience, underlining the need for Christian witness which rejects any appeal made on behalf of violence. The conversion has been complete: having been a lifelong pacifist by conviction, I have now gone through the additional revelation of having my pacifism confirmed by experience. I begin to appreciate St Augustine's (354–430) single-mindedness when he suggested that total abstinence is often less hazardous than perfect moderation.

As Christians committed to the standard of Christ, we have no alternative but to seek the complete conversion. There will be practical tensions in such a stance; but loyalty to Christ must needs be total, whereas obedience to the demands of the state can only be conditional. Absolute abstention where violence is concerned may look an awesome standard; yet, once adopted, it allows the Christian peacemaker to bring to the peace debate a dimension of credibility as much needed as it is vital.

This conviction, bringing together the pragmatic and the moral, has emerged as a key lesson from the Irish experience. We have learnt that violence delays and destroys the work of justice; we have been taught that there is no principled form of sinning; and we know that there is no principled way of killing. It cannot be otherwise: once we leave aside the pacifist model which is Christ, we lose both clarity of thought and moral authority in the argument. Worse still, we lapse into the spiritually sapping contradiction of trying to live with the Bible in one hand and the deterrent in the other.

The reversal of this process of compromise is one of today's Christian imperatives. In a polarised world, it is never easy to stand beside the pacifist Christ, but if Christian peacemakers do not take on the burden of explanation, who then is there to proclaim the totality of his love?

'Follow me' must be given full expression in the nuclear debate.

But the 'Bomb' is only the central symbol of today's peace debate – those who are caught up in 'limited' wars need also to be released from the fears of destruction. Effective peacemaking means a rejection of violence in *all* its forms, but, sadly, too many of those who oppose the 'Bomb' are seemingly unaware of the 'little bombs' which threaten much of humanity. In fact, those who ignore or condone 'lesser' weapons become fellow travellers with those who promote the nuclear club; and at the same time, as in Northern Ireland, they add greatly to the difficulties of peacemakers working in situations of communal strife.

All forms of violence (not only the 'Bomb') must be the focus of Christian concern. The hurling of an insult, the throwing of a stone, sectarian strife, economic injustice, the bullet or the petrol bomb – violent means, and all to be condemned as part of the destructive chain aiding and abetting nuclear madness. A vast agenda demanding daily dedication from individual pacifists.

When Irish friends ask for advice on personal witness, my response is usually: 'Do not allow the campaign of violence to destroy the divinely ordinary things of life. In particular, get on with the task of keeping the fabric of society together. Do what you would normally be doing for the good of the community, but do it with even more dedication.' So, Irish pacifists are encouraged to do what they can, when they can and where they can. A four-fold strategy is offered: pray peace, think peace, speak peace and act peace.

For the individual peacemaker in Ireland, perhaps the greatest challenge is that of being a bridge in a deeply divided community; here one is required to be a good counsellor, advocating reconciliatory attitudes with humility and consideration, knowing always that considerable sacrifices may be demanded from those addressed. In practice, the best of our individual peacemakers become agents of reconciliation in their own lives, witnessing alongside friends and neighbours. By entering into the tensions of their locality, peacemakers are enabled to express a living testimony which becomes the litmus test whereby wider proclamations may be made.

Peacemaking at such levels calls for a constant promotion of dialogue between contending groups. It is also important to discourage vocabularies of violence which, in an age of instant communication, can engender dangerous emotions. As we have learnt to our cost in Northern Ireland, insults like 'quisling', 'traitor', 'collaborator' provide the incitement and demented justification for terrible crimes against people and their property. For Christians in such situations, 'speak peace' takes on a new urgency.

But it is in collective 'act peace' initiatives that Christian peacemaking in Ireland has been most creative – and here the laity, co-operating across the sectarian divide have played a key role. The latest example of such inter-church co-operation is the Peace Education Programme for Schools in Ireland, sponsored by the Irish Council of Churches (Protestant) and the Irish Commission for Justice and Peace (Roman Catholic). This programme, unique in Europe for its range and ecumenical presentation, has courageously entered and survived a good many theological and historical-ecclesiological mine-fields. Remarkably, the programme has been approved and financed by churches, local and international, and by governments, north and south, in Ireland. It also has the support of teachers in both the Protestant and Catholic sectors.

In addition to formal classroom education, the 'beating of swords into ploughshares' is pursued in Northern Ireland through a multitude of community-based organisations dedicated to the peacemaking process. Most famous is the Corrymeela (Hill of Harmony) Centre, overlooking Ballycastle and the Atlantic Ocean in North Antrim (Colomba country). This complex of chalets and conference halls, built on seven acres of land, pre-dates the current 'troubles', but has grown up with and adapted to them. In the words of its founder and Director, Presbyterian Minister and veteran pacifist, Ray Davey: 'Reconciliation is the urgent job of all our churches today and here is common ground for all to work on. Corrymeela not only witnesses to this challenge, but is a symbol of it'.

Equally active are a host of interdenominational community organisations operating at the 'sharp end' of things and offering opportunities for a reconciling ministry. Women of the Cross, for example, is for mothers and wives who have lost a loved one in the conflict and who set out to comfort one another and to offer a releasing alternative to the bitterness which often accompanies grief; or, Soldiers of the Cross which was formed by converted-in-prison paramilitary terrorists, who sought to make reparation for their deeds by working for the conversion of their former terrorist associates, Protestant and Roman Catholic; or, most recently, the Columbanus Community of Reconciliation, sponsored by all the main churches as a residential community of Roman Catholics and Protestants 'committed to prayer and work for unity in the Church, justice in society and peace on earth'. It requires something of the faith of a St Columbanus to set forth on such a venture in Northern Ireland today; but the decision to found such an ecumenical community at such a time is proof of the powerful call which the search for Peace generates. These are only a few of the many Christians in Ireland who light candles, instead of cursing the darkness.

Greater hope, of course, would be felt if there were more signs of a political solution to Ireland's problems. Here we enter the greatest of all the mine-fields and the Church is required to step warily. The limitations on Church action politically are considerable, for just as Christians in Britain differ widely on important political issues, so in Ireland there is no specifically Christian policy on 'the Border issue' or whether Ireland should become a united republic or return to British sovereignty.

And how could it be otherwise? The Ulster and Irish 'questions' represent a complex human situation – a bewildering mix of rights and wrongs on all sides, a compound of historical forces, colonialism and political shortcomings, all culminating in a loss of direction which has brought about the disorientation of Northern Ireland's social fabric. The people of the Province, Protestant and Catholic alike, have been caught in one of history's hurricanes.

In this situation, the vital role of the Church is to encourage her people to engage in the reconciling process and to establish frameworks within which the forces of democratic dialogue can move towards a consensus.

The challenge to Christians becomes clear and unavoidable: it is to seek a formula which will make it possible for the considerable majority of Irish people in Northern Ireland (mainly Protestant) who value their British citizenship, to continue that citizenship in full; while at the same time, meeting the equally felt desire of another section of the North Irish people (mainly Roman Catholic) for guarantees which will enable them to enjoy equal status in the Northern Ireland state and aspire democratically and without penalty to an all-Ireland form of government.

Such a formula will be difficult to find, but it is the full measure of a problem which must be faced, which has been evaded for over sixty years and which until recently has all too rarely been 'taken aboard' by Irish and British churches in partnership. The Irish churches, straddling as they do the whole of Irish society and permeating the main political parties, are well placed to act as a creative catalyst. Indeed, the most constructive discussions that have taken place on the Anglo-Irish Agreement have been organised by Christian pacifist groupings.

And this is as it should be. Such issues are well suited to the strength of the churches in Ireland and to their place in the lives of the people. Moreover, they are precisely the sort of challenges to which Christians everywhere must respond if they are to remain a force for peace at the centre of contemporary life and mission.

The Episcopal
Peace Fellowship:
A Personal Perspective
John M. Gessell

THE agonising situation in which Christian pacifists and peacemakers exist today is the struggle for the fate of the earth and a struggle to remain faithful. Peacemaking is a confrontation with the strategy of death. The power and honour and glory of nations is construed, not in the greatness of a people, but in the organisation of power for death.

But peacemakers are animated by an alternative vision, a vision of God who discloses himself in history through Word and witness, calling into question all pretensions of national power. They must live biblically in the world between the Crucifixion and Resurrection.

> While we are still alive, we are surrendered into the hands of death for Jesus' sake, so that the life of Jesus may be revealed in our mortal body. So death is at work in us and life in you.
>
> (2 Cor. 4.11–12)

The ambivalent relationship between the Episcopal Church and the Episcopal Peace Fellowship can be understood in this context. In November 1939 the House of Bishops wrote: 'The Church in this hour must see to it that she . . . upholds above all national flags the Cross of a Christ, who belongs to no one nation or race.' And in their pastoral letter of October 1981, the Bishops wrote:

We are compelled to say that never before has it been so clear that reason forbids the use of violence, or the threat of it, as a means of securing one society against another. . . . With violence so deeply rooted in human behavior, it becomes an agony of growth to shift to another means of security. It remains far easier to rely on instruments of mutually assured destruction than to negotiate in patient non-violence for the means of mutually assured survival. *We are, therefore, prompted as religious leaders to impose upon ourselves the obligation for making this moral shift.* [emphasis added] We pray the Holy Spirit to change our hearts, moving us from violence to non-violence. We call upon our people to join us in that prayer.

This call for a 'moral shift' overturns 1,500 years of Christian moral theology, calls the Church into a new era of moral reflection on the nature of violence and non-violence and points the way to a new direction. But this call has not been met, one must confess, with alacrity. It remains both a bold and a cautious commitment. It does not make the EPF's agenda that of the Church, nor does it make of the Episcopal Church a peace church and it is not the central, animating principle in the Church's current peace programme. Although the EPF has been able over the last twelve years to put forward and to have accepted by General Convention some of its stated objectives in the form of resolutions and in the establishment of a Commission on Peace, the relationship has remained at arm's length. The Church is too involved in national economic and military policy to remain easy in the presence of its peace fellowship.

The Episcopal Pacifist Fellowship was born on Armistice Day 1939 in order to uphold the non-violent alternative, to support Episcopalians who, for conscience' sake, sought alternatives to military service, and to provide counselling for those who were perplexed about their Christian responsibility.

It was, as stated by Thomas Lee Hayes in his unpublished history of the EPF,

> to raise up before the life of the Episcopal Church, and to act more truly as it believed the Christian Church must, that high adventure of living under the Cross rather than following only a particular national flag, however worthy of honor and allegiance that flag may be.

The Bishops had said, 'War as an instrument of national policy is a denial of God.' The EPF would focus its spotlight on the Episcopal Church itself, thus the personal and corporate witness for the pacifist position was embodied in the earliest and foundational days of the organisation.

From those early days, the EPF was concerned to focus on peace-making as a positive alternative to war-making. The early Episcopal pacifists included among their numbers many well-known persons, such as John Nevin Sayre and Bishop W. Appleton Lawrence. While some notable women also associated themselves with the newly formed fellowship, the dominant EPF leadership in those early years was drawn from 'big guns'(!) in the Church, largely (though not entirely) white, Anglo-Saxon males. Thus it was accepted within the establishment and its voice was included in some notable statements made by General Convention and the House of Bishops.

Following the Second World War, in an effort to include those who could not honestly call themselves 'pacifists', the organisation changed itself into the Episcopal Peace Fellowship.

The second phase of EPF history had its beginning, of course, with the Vietnam War. It was at this time that EPF came into its own as a national peace group with a full programme and staff. And, as Tom Hayes writes, 'it also meant having to deal with the ambiguities of being an active anti-war organisation.' EPF became involved in the anti-war movements, the civil rights movement, concerns for economic and social justice, including women's issues and the death penalty. It made common cause with other groups within the Episcopal Church who were struggling for some of the same ends.

By some measurements, EPF has had a better track record influencing Church policy since 1967 than before. The 1967 General Convention, meeting in Seattle, failed to address the issues of the war in Vietnam. Since that time EPF concerns have fared consistently better in General Convention. In 1982, the Convention resolved that this Church

> urges members . . . to consider resisting war by such non-violent means as conscientious refusal to participate in any war, refusal to register for the draft, refusal of induction orders, prayer vigils at or within military or other war-related facilities, refusal to pay war-related taxes and other peaceful acts of war resistence.

And in 1985, General Convention established a Standing Commission on Peace to develop recommendations and strategies which will be of concrete assistance to the Church in furthering the work of issues of peace and justice. This was the culmination of a seven-year effort of the EPF National Executive Committee to build a peace programme into the structures of the Church itself. In addition to conceptualising and helping to bring about a permanent commission on peace, the EPF also raised the money, organised and sponsored the first national Church peace conference in 1982. It was attended by representatives of about one-third of the dioceses of the Church. The conference has since been sponsored by the Executive Council staff of the Church itself. While EPF has continued to press the Church on peace issues and to support draft resisters by various means, the mood of the Church has not always been welcoming. At times, there has appeared to be resistance to informing young persons of their draft alternatives. At times, EPF has been distanced by some of the official Church and, occasionally, has been subject to extravagant criticism.

In the United States today under the Reagan administration, the nuclear arms race must be viewed, not merely as foreign and military policy, but as a secular faith response of a certain kind translated into politics of a most deadly sort. Peacemaking as the believer's response, then, takes place in a highly politicised context, where the superordinate claims of the state are becoming increasingly apparent day by day. But peacemaking cannot be merely a rival political strategy. If it is so construed, we will all miss the point. It is a rival faith commitment which must be acted out in the disciplines of regular Bible study, theological reflection, prayer and action. The situation of rival faith claims should shape EPF's response in the future.

It is in this light that EPF has recently undertaken to inaugurate a Covenant Ministry of Resistance and Reconciliation. This is a call to a *community of resistance*. It is independent of any official Church programme and it is a significant focus of EPF's work for justice and peace at all levels. It is hoped that such a community of resistance will embody a stance that truly affirms and embraces prophetic resistance to war and violence. I see this as the future vocation of EPF in the Church and in the national community.

Pacifism and the Nuclear Debate

Bruce Kent

IT would be all too easy to suggest that theories about pacifism need to have little to do with the nuclear debate. After all, does it matter how an individual comes to reject nuclear weapons and all weapons of mass destruction? Whether one wanders painfully through the complicated thickets of just war theories or whether one moves in one leap to a pacifist position, we Christians ought to end up in much the same place. For it seems to me, and to many Christians, that it is quite impossible to justify nuclear weapons under the moral umbrella of just war theories. At the very least, such weapons – and that is not the right name for them since weapons are meant to defend and not to destroy the defender – are indiscriminate in their effects. No other 'weapon' kills the innocent of future generations. The radioactive fall-out resulting from the smallest nuclear explosion above ground will continue to have its deadly effects for years to come. As I write, the world stands in fear of the consequences of one small nuclear disaster in a Soviet reactor. It is said that the effects of that accident were equivalent to the detonation of one kiloton bomb. There are bombs of that size and some even smaller, but many, many of the warheads deployed today are vastly more powerful. Few knowledgeable people, in any event, now suggest that nuclear war can be limited to single explosions. The authoritative Palme Commission report of 1982, *Common Security*, said that to assume a limited nuclear war

> one must make incredible assumptions about the rationality of decision makers under intense pressure, about the resilience of the people and the machinery in command and control systems, about

social coherence in the face of unprecedented devastation and suffering . . . it all strains even the imagination . . . the underlying dynamic would almost inevitably propel the conflict into larger and larger proportions.

In short, it is only because we have forgotten how restrictive even just war conditions were and are and have persisted in thinking of nuclear weapons in inadequate ways because our minds cannot imagine the damage they can do, that we have failed to draw the obvious conclusions. Whatever may be said of the deterrent threat, any use of nuclear weapons is for a Christian impossible if that Christian is trying to do justice to traditional Christian thinking on issues of war and peace.

There are, of course, some serious practical and moral problems about the deterrent threat itself. No threat can be very credible if the penalty supposed to be backing it up is morally not an option for the one who threatens. Moreover, Jesus Christ was as concerned with out hearts and our intentions as with our acts. To threaten to commit mass murder ('population extermination', Julian Critchley MP once said of Polaris policies) even if one hopes and believes that the threat will never have to be carried out, is itself a profound corruption of the human spirit.

If these conclusions are fairly reasonable, and more and more non-pacifist Christians seem to think that they are, why are Christian pacifists and Christian non-pacifists not holding hands together rather more enthusiastically than at present appears? After all, following different roads, we ought to come to very similar conclusions.

Part of the reason lies with the pacifists. True, they have been given a bad image for a long time. Showing how disloyal, silly, illogical and impractical they are has been fair game for lots of 'reasonable' Christian people. A Catholic Truth Society pamphlet was published well after the Second World War in which the clerical author stated with conviction that 'Jesus Christ would not have been such a fool as to have been a pacifist.' Pacifists do not protect their innocent neighbours; pacifists let evil people run over them and others with hobnailed boots; pacifists, in short, are passive! Some very odd ideas about pacifists were in general circulation for a very long time and still are now. We still lack a nice crunchy English word for 'active non-violence' and one really has to deliver a short sermon on Martin Luther King, Helder Camara and Dorothy Day before one can put different flesh on pacifist bones. For far too long, pacifism has been identified with weakness, wetness and lack of moral fibre.

There is of course another problem: pacifists have a strong tendency to sound and be judgemental and self-righteous. As one of them, I know the temptation. Only the other day, a pacifist friend of mine, in front of a rather sleepy looking military base, was storming up and down with 'Hypocrisy!' popping out of his mouth from time to time. Not the best way to win friends and influence people, I fear. It can get worse. I am really tired of the pacifist tendency to excommunicate. That used to be an operation reserved to popes and they did not make, often enough, a very good job of it. Pacifist excommunication can be even more arbitrary. 'How can anyone call themselves a Christian unless they renounce all violence?' goes up the outraged cry. Well the fact is that they do, they are in good conscience and they are on a road which has had Christian footsteps on it since the time of Constantine (d.337).

The effect on such people of the strictures of the purist pacifist is anger or boredom or both. Chopping people off may provide emotional satisfaction, but it does not persuade and it builds no bridges. To build bridges in the Christian world is desperately important. A common front, at least in opposition to weapons of mass destruction, ought to be perfectly possible. In such a building process, the pragmatic pacifists like myself have an important part to play. I was not brought up with pacifism. I'm sure that the words 'coward' and 'conscientious objector' would have been closely associated in my mind. I enjoyed (oops!) my military service. That I might ever have had to refuse an order never crossed my mind. Mine was the world of Kipling, P.C. Wren and *The Charge of the Light Brigade*. None of this conflicted in any way with my Catholic Christianity which actually, since the days of my school cadet corps, reinforced such attitudes. We were, after all, on the side of Right. To fight for one's country was a noble Christian duty. To question government policy was disloyal and even treasonable. We did not know it, but Caesar had, as a result of centuries of Church/state partnership, been allowed to take far more than his proper share of our lives.

My own process of change was a gradual one; it took many years. As the result of personal contact with a few great (non-pacifist) Christians like the late Archbishop Thomas Roberts SJ, I came early in the 1960s, too late to be involved with the first wave of CND, to judge that nuclear weapons had to be rejected. It was a joy to me, though it seemed to have little effect on Church attitudes to government policies, when the Second Vatican Council clearly condemned the use of weapons of mass destruction. But it was a long time after that before I came to think of myself as a pacifist. Perhaps the futility and dreadful starvation deaths of the Nigerian War, a conflict about which I came to know quite a lot, helped me to believe that killing solves no problems; it only creates new ones. At the same time I came to understand that the pacifist who is not concerned with social justice is no pacifist at all. It was Pope Paul VI in *Populorum Progressio* who once said that 'Peace is the fruit of anxious daily care to see that all people live in the justice that God intends.' One of the main weaknesses in pacifism *as perceived* is that it seems to concern itself only with the issues of killing or not killing. The perception is happily not always a correct one. The Society of Friends, understood by many to be the example of a Christian pacifist group, is clearly very concerned in the most practical ways with bringing to an end, not only the violence of open warfare and bloody conflict, but the situations of structural injustice so often responsible for that violence.

The Christian pacifist has really three choices. He or she can reject the institutional Church altogether on the grounds that it is irredeemable. Others may not choose such a radical option, but can retire into what can only be described as self-righteous isolation. Some, in this spirit, do not leave the Church, but regularly suggest that those who do not agree with them are either in bad faith or gross ignorance. Theirs is the spirit of excommunication. The third option seems to me to make much more sense. It is to do all one can to help the mass of our fellow Christians to move towards a position of active non-violence and work for social justice, which membership of a community which professes One Father has to involve.

The great American social reformer, Saul Alinsky, said repeatedly that people do not move forward if they cannot find a way to start. The hunt for first steps is the vital one. For many Christians, those steps are to be found in the linkage between the arms race and world poverty. Many simply do not know the details of Britain's own active arms export industry – or realise that institutional churches, through their investment holdings, can be actively engaged in it. People soon realise that there is not much point raising laborious funds for some Third World project while a government-backed arms industry is milking the country concerned of funds which it could itself be using for constructive purposes. The pacifist should be actively looking for those triggers which lead to first steps. As Einstein once said, it is because in the nuclear age we have not learned to change our 'modes of thinking' that we drift towards unparalleled disaster. Christians can get very stuck in their unquestioning assumptions. They, for the most part, still give to national loyalty a priority not justified by the gospel. They know almost nothing of the limits of warfare imposed by international law. They still think of wars today as if they could be 'won'. They still apply two standards of moral judgement – one to the west and another to the east. They still think that nuclear deterrence is more or less a stable system of security. They believe that some merit is to be found in nuclear 'parity' or 'balance', as if we were still dealing in Spitfires and Messerschmitts. Unhappily, both in schools and parishes there is an almost total ignorance about the workings and reports of the United Nations. In our churches – committed as they ought to be to the vision of what the United Reformed Church once called the 'transnational Body of Christ' – I have yet to come across a Diocesan United Nations Education Secretary, for instance. Too often, when I ask a group of Christian sixth formers or university students if any have read the great 1978 United Nations report on disarmament and the arms race, I find out that they have never even heard of it.

In short, the pacifist has a vision of a healing, reconciling, justice-building Christianity in which he or she wants others to share. That means a great deal of dialogue. It is *not* the business of the comfortable European pacifist to pass judgement on others forced to awful choices. What would I *really* do if, in some rural area of Nicaragua, I discovered Contras in the process of butchering my family?

It *is* our pacifist business to unite with our fellow Christians as we try to build a world where the peace of Christ is a little more obvious and where love of enemies means taking practical steps. In this nuclear age, with all our fragile planet at risk, there is no more important task. Pragmatic pacifists have a great part to play in it.

Women's Perspective on War and Peace

Valerie Flessati and Clare Prangley

WHAT we are going to offer you in this chapter is the fruit of several workshops which we have led with groups of women and men at Pax Christi international meetings on peace, spirituality and non-violence.

As Christians concerned about world peace, we are aware that our relationship with God and how it is integrated into our daily lives in our commitment to the Kingdom does not take place in a vacuum. Believing in the Incarnation, we know that our 'bodily' and 'spiritual' lives cannot be separated. God entered history in Jesus and was subject to the cultural, social and religious patterns of his time. Through the Resurrection he transcended history and liberated us all, but this was only possible through his living out of the Good News in his particular historical context and in a sinful and fallen world.

When we talk of women's perspective on peace, we are not talking of something which is distinctive because of women's *nature*. Genesis 1.27 makes it clear that men and women are made equally in the image of God; there is no hierarchy, which, according to the Bible, enters the world with the Fall. The Old Testament prophets are recalling Israel to a faithfulness which has nothing to do with strength against enemies in men and weaponry, or even prayers and sacrifice, but is about doing *justice* to all the oppressed in their society, which included widows and orphans (Isa. 1.11–17). Women are included with the foreigner, the poor and the hungry on the margins of society.

Anything distinctive in women's perspective on peace and war comes from their *experience* of life, rather than from any notion that women are somehow more pacific than men, with qualities 'naturally' separating the sexes by rigid definition: man the warrior, woman the home-maker. Do we not all know men who are tender, compassionate, dependent or illogical, and women who are competitive, tough, incisive or aggressive?

The particular set of experiences lived by women throughout history, often shaped by the stereotyped expectations, has made it easier perhaps for them to make certain connections. After all, one is more likely to see the flaws in a system in which one has little stake. They are recognising that the classic dualism of man-reason-spiritual transcendence/woman-intuition-corporal-chained to earth, results in exploitation, rape and oppression of all kinds: not just sexism, but racism, north-south injustice, ecological irresponsibility and holocaust. Identification of others as 'non-persons' leads, ultimately, to the horrors of the nuclear age.

What large numbers of women, active now in the peace movement of the 1980s have come to see, with anger and shock, has been aptly expressed by the American Benedictine, Sr Joan Chittister: 'Half of the people of the world are going to be exterminated by the nuclear wars that men are designing to protect them, and nobody's even going to ask us if that's allright.' It is this awareness that has propelled thousands of women of all ages to become vigorous peace campaigners, taking on unaccustomed roles in public speaking, political lobbying, statistical and scientific research, or non-violent civil disobedience, in a widespread revolt against the threat of nuclear war and the forces leading towards it.

In trying to analyse the elements in women's perspective on and contribution to peace and war, we are using something like the well-tried See-Judge-Act method of the Young Christian Workers tradition. What we *see* are a number of experiences common to many women across the world and throughout history, including such things as the experience of exclusion, powerlessness and guilt. In the light of experience, we *judge* the situation by reflecting on the many parallels to be found in Scripture, and discover that Jesus himself identified with outcasts and chose to suffer the fate of the guilty and the powerless as an innocent victim. Lastly, we consider how women *act* in the peace movement today, taking as our chief example the best-known current model in peace campaigning, the Greenham Common women's peace camp, where, whether they share this Christian analysis or not, the lives of women are echoing the messages that come through Scripture and bearing witness to the new Jerusalem where 'every tear will be wiped away' (Rev. 21.4).

WATCHING AND WAITING

This is one of the simplest but most common experiences of women. Watching over a sick child, waiting for birth, for death, at the cradle or at the Cross, it is women's experience to simply *be there*. It involves faithfulness and rugged endurance, hours of patient anxiety and sleeplessness in times of crisis. At Calvary, it was the faithfulness of the watching women which proved stronger than the fear of the male apostles who ran away.

In the past, women had to wait passively for men to come home from war, from the Front. In the next war this will not happen. And so today, women at Greenham are employing the functions of watching and waiting in a preventative capacity. By physically being there at the gates, day in and day out, in all weathers, winter and summer alike, they have played an absolutely crucial role, faithfully watching out for Cruise missiles, both before they arrived and since. By alerting others, they are the essential core to the wider Cruisewatch network which monitors and follows every movement of the missiles. By putting their bodies on the spot, Greenham women are an enduring protest ('like a tree standing by the water, we shall not be moved') which has proved impossible to uproot.

EXCLUSION

So many provinces in life have by tradition been closed to women, that few of us have not known what it feels like to be excluded – from particular professions, clubs, sports, the decision-making levels at work or in society and, of course, from many aspects of Church life, including even the language of prayer. The achievements of women have been kept invisible, their names unknown and their contributions underrated. Despite suffrage, actual decision making about military and political matters has remained almost entirely in the hands of men. In the courts, women are judged by men; in hospitals, they are treated by men; their psychological problems are defined by men; their financial undertakings have to be ratified by men and their religious lives are regulated by men.

Things were no different in the time of Jesus, who chose to exclude himself from respectability by identifying with the outcasts. There was critical reaction from the men around him when Jesus allowed a sinful woman to touch him, even in the humblest gesture of anointing his feet (Luke 7.36–50). He exposed the hypocrisy of the Pharisees who tried to get him to support their double standards in judging the woman caught in adultery and condemning her to death (John 8.3–11). Even the apostles refused to accept first-hand evidence from the women who had received the Easter message at the empty tomb (Luke 24.11). The evidence of women was inadmissible; it did not count.

At Greenham, exclusion is powerfully symbolised by the perimeter fence, periodically reinforced with extra layers of razor wire to keep women out and clearly define which side one is on. On the women's side there is exclusion, too, not just from the comfort of home, but from all the most basic facilities. The right to shelter, caravans and tents, has been removed, and, at different times, other rights have been withdrawn or threatened: camp fires, water supplies, post and even voting rights. The women have been excluded from the protection of the police, as harassment and physical attacks by local thugs have been overlooked. By acting outside stereotyped female behaviour, they have been abused as unfeminine and treated as though they have somehow excluded themselves from the human race and most especially from the female species. There has been hardly any constructive debate about the issues they are raising. It has almost all focused on deriding them *as women*.

POWERLESSNESS – EMPOWERING OTHERS

The widespread exclusion of women from the systems which govern our society and its decisions on matters of life and death – 'and nobody's even going to ask us if that's all right' – has given many of them a sense of powerlessness: that there's nothing they can do to affect things. Overnight, changes are made which can make a profound difference to their lives. Prices go up, allowances are cut, but the demands on the family housekeeping budget remain the same. School, hospital and transport services diminish, yet there always seems to be enough money for Cruise,

Trident and new fighter planes. Women quickly make the connections.

So powerlessness goes together, paradoxically, with empowerment, as their determined and righteous anger propels them to take action. Just as they are used to encouraging young people to grow up, gain their independence and discover their own skills, so now they encourage each other to take the difficult steps to break out of powerless passivity into powerful collective action.

The paradox of power and powerlessness is a central mystery in the gospels, too, where time and again the worldly view of power is turned upside down. Real power belongs to the baby born in the poverty of the stable, and in the ultimate model of non-violent suffering: the undeserved execution of death on the Cross. We treasure the Magnificat and the Beatitudes in which we learn that the Godly use of power is, quite clearly, to uphold the powerless. Those who are hungry will be fed, those who mourn comforted, the mighty cast from their thrones and the rich sent away empty, in a complete reversal of normal practice in our society. They provide us with a tremendous source of hope and empowerment which is reinforced by Jesus' affirmation of the Samaritan woman, the woman who anointed his head and the Resurrection witnesses as bearers of the Good News.

Sarah Hipperson, one of the long-term residents at the Greenham peace camp, has spoken movingly of the paradox of power she has experienced there. The women are powerless in the conventional sense, easy to throw on one side when a gate is blocked, a small, physically weak band when faced by an organised rank of uniformed policemen. And yet, committed as they are to non-violence whatever the provocation, the *real* power – the psychological, moral and spiritual strength – lies with the women. This is borne out by the fact that the police have to get 'psyched up' as a group, into a more aggressive frame of mind in order to approach and challenge them.

Officials, reporters and visitors have been mystified by the lack of a conventional power structure in the women's peace movement. No apparent leaders, shared decision making and a refusal to dominate have been marked features of the way events have been organised, with an emphasis on the valued contribution of each participant.

The empowerment of other women, which has attracted even

grandmothers who never would have dreamed before that they would ever encircle a military base, may prove the longest-lasting legacy of Greenham. Women all over the country – indeed, all over the world – have felt its effects, in that it is now all right for them to admit to their 'emotional' feelings of sorrow, anger, extreme fear, anxiety, and waste at the prospect of nuclear annihilation. These have become respectable reasons to act and to demand a different basis for international relations.

Power at Greenham, as in the non-violent Cross, resides in the willingness of some to make substantial sacrifices in order to witness to the truth and to save the rest of creation.

BEING MADE TO FEEL GUILTY

It is a frequent tactic of human beings in our male-dominated society to project guilt onto women. If relationships fail, women feel that there must be something wrong with *them*. If children are wayward, we say their mothers brought them up badly. If a woman is raped, we ask what she was wearing and what she was doing out so late at night. We don't ask what *he* was doing on the streets in that part of town and suggest that other men stay in after dark lest they be similarly tempted.

'It was the woman you put with me; she gave me the fruit and I ate it' said Adam (Gen. 3.12) trying to put the blame onto Eve. Making woman responsible for the Fall initiated centuries of insult and inferiority which are with us still. 'The gateway to the devil' (Tertullian), women were regarded as ritually unclean, intended for distasteful and base functions like childbearing, along with all the attendant bodily duties: cleaning, feeding, nursing, which would otherwise distract men from spiritual, intellectual and more godly aspirations.

The primary accusations levelled against the women at Greenham are no more sophisticated than this. They are blamed for living in a squalid mess, for being unfeminine, for being lesbians (used derogatively to imply those whom no man would want to go near) and for neglecting their husbands and children by leaving their homes. Such accusations would never be made of a soldier doing what was seen to be his duty. Living in the mud of trenches and undergrowth is unpleasant and dirty, and requires considerable sacrifice. But no one would question this, or the necessity for a man to leave his wife and children in time of war. Yet to these women the pain and sacrifice of discomfort and separation are worthwhile because they know they are doing all they can to secure their children's future by trying to *prevent* the next war. Joan Baez has made the military comparison:

> I would say that I'm a non-violent soldier. In place of weapons of violence, you have to use your mind, your heart, your sense of humour, every faculty available to you . . . because no one has the right to take the life of another human being.

The most perverse accusation occurs when Greenham women are the ones who are charged with 'breaching the peace' and blamed for defiling the Common – as though the military base itself does not do that in far greater measure! It reminds one of the old enclosures rhyme:

> The law condemns the man or woman
> Who steals the goose from off the common
> But lets the greater felon loose
> Who steals the common from the goose.

SOLIDARITY

Although the stereotype depicts women in spiteful rivalry and competition, women more usually experience strong bonds of mutual support which span the generations, particularly when facing the misfortunes of life. We see such solidarity in the gospels in the visit of Mary to her older cousin, Elizabeth, like herself pregnant for the first time. It is a compassionate solidarity which extends in the Magnificat to a bias, or 'preferential option' towards the poor and oppressed, lifting up the lowly and filling the hungry with good things (Luke 1.46–55). The family bond and essential unity of all human beings is summed up in the prayer taught us by Jesus himself (Matt. 6.9–15). If God is 'Our Father', our solidarity must be with all our sisters and brothers, beyond the man-made divisions of race, creed, language or nation.

This kind of solidarity is expressed in the women's peace movement by an emphasis on shared tasks and decision making, and by attempts to ensure that the immediate community is built up with warmth and friendship as a prerequisite for confronting together the evil face of militarism. Honest, just and peaceful relationships on the personal level go together with pursuing just and peaceful relationships in the wider world. The personal is political and one action is linked with another.

For many women, Greenham has taken on a spiritual significance as a place of safety or sanctuary, as a 'woman's space' to which in a sense women can retreat, both to be healed from and to heal, wounds inflicted by a violent society. Violence is the product of the enhancement and glorification of the *macho* image in our culture, which is encouraged and fostered in a thousand different ways, however much violence may be denounced in words.

The spider's web is a symbol often employed by the women to denote the interconnectedness of people and of issues. It has been a principal objective of the peace movement of the 1980s to try to expose and understand these links more fully. We know from United Nations' and other studies, how vital is the link between development and disarmament: that the resources, research and cash so urgently needed to solve the world's health, environmental and food problems, are wasted on the never-satiated appetite of arms research and development. We know, too, that of the world's poor, women are always the poorest and the last to gain when any advantages do filter down. Although an estimated 500 million adult women in the world are still illiterate, the education of women has been found to be the most important factor influencing the survival rates of their children. The infant mortality rate in countries where women's literacy is lowest is eight times that of countries where women's literacy rates are highest (Ruth Leger Sivard: *World Military and Social Expenditures 1985*).

It is awareness of these connections that has led women in the peace movement to make special efforts to arrange visits and to listen to the voices of sisters in the Pacific region, Southern Africa, the Soviet Union, Japan, Central and Latin America, with all of whom we form one global family, concerned for the health and welfare of all our children. Such international networking could be truly subversive to future war preparations, as more and more women come to echo the words of Virginia Woolf: 'As a woman I have no country . . . as a woman my country is the whole world'. (*Three Guineas*, 1938)

INFERIORITY UNDER THE LAW OF MEN

In biblical times, as has already been mentioned, the testimony of women did not count in law and the apostles were not prepared to believe that such important news as that of the

Resurrection could have been entrusted to women, who must have been mistaken. Jesus upheld the law, but he corrected its distortions, saying that the law was made to serve people, not the other way round. By imposing his law of love, he freed us from the burdens of distorted legal pedantry and this is a particularly welcome gift to women, against whom the law has often been used in this way: one rule for men, another for women.

In recent years, the trials of thousands of peace activists, many of them Greenham women, have revealed the inadequacy of the legal system even today when it comes to admitting evidence which goes beyond the narrow limits of the minor national laws which defendants have infringed. Many defendants have appealed to international law to show that the reason for their 'crimes' is to draw attention to the higher laws of humanity which are being broken by our preparation to wage nuclear war – nothing less than an international criminal conspiracy to commit genocide. Greenham women even took the United States to court under international law to challenge the deployment of Cruise missiles in Europe. It was not held admissible, but every such action helps to hasten the day when we will have competent and effective international legal mechanisms to protect all of life on earth, overriding the claims of the idol of national sovereignty.

CREATIVITY AND LIFEGIVING

> There is no battlefield on earth, nor ever has been, howsoever covered with slain, which it has not cost the women of the race more in actual bloodshed and anguish to supply, than it has cost the men who lie there. We pay the first cost on all human life . . . No woman who is a woman says of a human body, 'It is nothing!'
>
> (*Woman and Labour*, 1911)

So wrote Olive Schreiner, one of the first generation of this century's women peacemakers. She goes to the heart of women's perspective on war and peace, for if women share so immediately the labour of creating life, they must surely be in a position to know its real value. This should make it that much harder for women to accept disembodied calculations estimating several million casualties as 'unavoidable losses' after even a 'limited' nuclear exchange.

The unspeakable suffering of Japanese women A-Bomb survivors who faced a life of enforced celibacy or perpetual anxiety about the health risks to their children, born and unborn, puts before us very starkly the solemn biblical choice. 'I have set before you life and death, blessings and curses. Now choose life, so that you and your children may live' (Deut. 30.19). This is for us today a deliberate choice in the way that it has never been before, for women in centuries past had no control over the diseases, poor hygiene and malnutrition which robbed them of their children. Personal and collective conversion is urgently needed if we are to choose rightly, rejecting the false gods of nationalism and militarism, and seeking our security in the creative God of new and more abundant life.

The forces of violence and evil have such a grip on our culture that we have great difficulty even imagining and articulating a creative concept of peace as an attractive and challenging proposition. It is to start remedying this that women have developed positive symbols and activities to accompany the negative opposition of much peace campaigning. Planting seeds, dancing on silos, singing, weaving and new ways of organising are all features which emphasise life and the hoped-for survival of our beautiful planet.

At Greenham and the other bases, the wire fence presents the life/death choice most vividly. Inside it, one sees ugly buildings, noisy aircraft, soldiers who are trained to avoid normal human exchange with the subversive women, while scrubby hillocks hide the deadly missiles themselves. Along the fence on the outside, carefully nurtured daffodils pathetically proclaim different values. At Comiso in Sicily, the long rows of vines and other abundant crops stop abruptly within feet of the fence protecting the missiles. The visual message is obvious: the works of death are a brutal interruption of the works of mercy; of the way human beings are meant to live – beneath their vines and their fig trees, and unafraid. It is the hope of women in the peace movement today that, by bringing to it the fresh approach arising from their particular experiences of life, they will be adding a dimension hitherto missing, a perspective and contribution which, together with that of their brothers, will hasten the advent of the prophetic vision of peace for which we all pray.

3

CHANGING
THE
WORLD

How do we actually go about living the gospel of peace?

If campaigning, what happens when campaigners use methods of which the government disapproves? What methods are valid? Individual questions and answers change people's minds. They could even influence future governments. It is essential to break down barriers between potentially hostile peoples. Is your town or church 'twinned' with anywhere in Eastern Europe? Perhaps you could travel there. Young people could seriously consider voluntary work camps . . .

What about the next generation? Is the way we bring up our children, both at home and at school, really conducive to peace?

Finally, what about the established Church? A reasoned plea for action, with tolerance.

Non-violent
Direct Action
Barbara Eggleston

ON Ash Wednesday 1986, a group of Christians gathered outside the Ministry of Defence building in Whitehall, London. This group, Catholic Peace Action, regularly holds vigils and services at this place. They leaflet the workers and have engaged in correspondence with various individual civil servants. On this occasion, the traditional Ash Wednesday liturgy was to be accompanied by an act of civil disobedience, during which eight people – myself included – would mark the walls of the MOD building with crosses and the word 'REPENT' written in blessed ash. This symbolic action – a call to our nation to repent of its dependence on weapons of mass destruction – led to eight people being arrested and charged with Criminal Damage. It led to a court case, during which the magistrate discussed deterrence and peace, and during which morality and justice were raised as important matters for the court.

This is only one of many actions that have taken place in this country over the past few years. Many Christians have engaged in acts of non-violent direct action which have led to arrest and even imprisonment. This is not just a British phenomenon. In the United States, actions by many people, including priests, have led to some very heavy prison sentences. Currently, there are four Christians serving sentences of up to twenty-four years for damaging a missile silo lid. Other Christians have been prosecuted for providing sanctuary for refugees from Central America.

This is not a new departure for Christian peace and justice activists. During the 1960s, Christians were arrested in the US for burning draft cards or evading call-up to the war in Vietnam. In South Africa, Christians have been imprisoned for disobeying the laws of Apartheid and for supporting banned organisations such as the ANC. We have seen this thread throughout history. There have always been some Christians who choose to disobey the laws of the state in order to obey the authority of their God and their faith. In this chapter, I will be looking at this phenomenon and its Christian justification.

In the past, Christian peacemakers would divide themselves into two groups: pacifists and just war theorists. Both could wait for the outbreak of war to apply their principles. Pacifists, with their moral commitment never to fight, would be conscientious objectors and refuse to be involved in the war effort. Advocates of just war principles would choose to oppose specific acts of war, or particular wars which they held to be unjust, for example, those that involved the bombing of civilians.

In the nuclear age it is too late to wait for the outbreak of war to express dissent. Principles have to be acted on now, while they still have meaning, if not they become irrelevant.

Non-violent direct action is a way of expressing dissent now, while it matters. It can be used as a term to refer to all public types of witness, including legal strikes and demonstrations. Within the peace movement, however, it is more usually used to refer to those actions that involve some element of law breaking and it can also be called civil disobedience.

Some civil disobedience is purely symbolic: a sign of dissent. Those people who continue to decorate the fences of Greenham or Molesworth are breaking the military by-laws: this is civil disobedience, a way of saying that the authority that invoked this law is not going to silence those who wish to protest. The Snowball campaign is another symbolic campaign aiming to persuade the government to take disarmament seriously. Until the campaign's demands are met, Snowballers openly cut one strand of wire at nuclear bases and then give themselves up to the police. The numbers involved increase – snowball – from action to action.

There can be more direct action, such as attempting to close a base by blockading, or by hindering a Cruise convoy exercise. There can be actions that involve worship at places declared out of bounds by the military authorities; thereby confronting the 'idols' of this age with true worship and putting into practice the call in the Book of Common Prayer to worship *'at all times, and in all places'*. There is also tax resistance: the refusal to pay the proportion of tax for military or nuclear purposes. There are actions whose purpose is to make known evil – often in dramatic ways – such as many of the events organised by Greenpeace.

Many people question the effectiveness of such action. Recently, Cory Aquino's victory in the Philippines came about after peaceful direct action by thousands of ordinary people who, in contravention of martial law, came onto the streets and literally put their bodies between the pro-Marcos army and the so-called 'rebels' to prevent an army massacre. It became known as People Power! Refusal to conform to unjust law was also seen during the Nazi occupation of Europe. In Denmark, Jews were saved from the death camps by the mass refusal of the Danes to conform with anti-Semitic legislation. In Norway, school teachers successfully resisted Nazi attempts to interfere with school curricula. We know of other campaigns: Mahatma Gandhi's struggle for Indian independence, Martin Luther King's civil rights campaign, the suffragettes, action to help secure votes for women.

These were all campaigns against unjust laws, often in oppressive societies. But civil disobedience also has a place in societies that lay claim to the title of democracy. Even in democracies unjust laws can exist and evils can hide under the shield of legality. Citizens can also be rendered powerless by the force of big corporations and state power.

In 1981, in France, the farmers of the Larzac region won their long campaign of civil disobedience against the military take over of their land. In the 1970s, Cesar Chavez in California led a long campaign of strikes, pickets and boycotts for the union rights of agricultural workers. There are also examples of 'effective' action nearer home. When the United States first planned to deploy land-based Cruise missiles in Europe, their vision was of a weapon that would 'melt into the countryside'. The women camped outside the gates of Greenham Common airbase have ensured that these weapons do not leave the base unnoticed, and Cruisewatch monitors each deployment, following the convoys and holding protests along the routes to the dispersal sites. There has been no secret, silent deployment. The invisible has been made visible.

Evil often prospers behind the mask of acceptability. We should not forget that over the main gate of Auschwitz was the sign, 'Work makes free' – dressing up the horrors of the final solution in more respectable clothes. One of the effects of the peace actions at military bases in Britain has been to strip away the acceptable mask. Bases are no longer visually what they were. They no longer look benign – barbed wire, razor wire, watch-towers, Alsatian dogs. The mask has come down and they now look like what they are – death camps. This is a vital process in building the wider movement, for it enables people to see what is being built and planned in their names and with their money.

RENDER UNTO CAESAR

Can there possibly be religious, as opposed to political, justification for acts of civil disobedience? Frequently, those involved in actions are offered biblical quotes to persuade them that Christian faith requires obedience to the state, and that Jesus would never have been involved in the type of actions that they find themselves in.

Taken out of context, Romans 13 would appear to rule out any act of lawbreaking by Christians: 'Let every person be subject to the governing authorities . . . he who resists the authorities resists what God has appointed' (13.1, 2). To read this passage in this way would be to ignore both its context and the actual example of its author, St Paul. Paul is the man referred to in the second letter to Timothy as 'suffering and wearing fetters like a criminal' (2.9) and the man who wrote the letter to the Philippians from prison. None of the apostles obeyed all laws regardless. They did not consider the secular law to be above challenge, but they did believe that law was important and that Christians should play their part where possible in secular society, as long as this did not involve idolatry. Peter's statement before the council, after his arrest, that 'We must obey God rather than men' (Acts 5.29) continues the thread laid down by Jesus in his discourse about the payment of tax to Caesar: 'Render to Caesar the things that are Caesar's, and to God the things that are God's' (Mark 12.17). It would appear that for Jesus, obedience to secular authority was to be judged within the demands of God's higher authority. When the state plays God, we are to withdraw our support or fall into idolatry.

This view has historically been the view of the Church. As Thomas Aquinas stated in his *Summa*, 'When the Emperor commands one thing and God another, one should ignore the former and obey the latter' (Q. 104, Art. 5). And there is Thomas More's famous defence: 'I am the King's good servant, but God's first'. Throughout history, Christians have fallen into idolatry by confusing God and Caesar. The result is always tragic. The Apartheid state, like the Nazi state, raises the idol of racial purity whose worship leads to injustice and terror. Without resistance from Christians, worship itself becomes tainted with idolatry and ceases to truly preach the gospel.

And today, we in Britain live in a national security state, which aims at protecting its global economic privilege through the threat and, if necessary, the use of weapons of genocide. Our strength – nuclear and economic – has become an idol.

Non-violent action and civil disobedience in our society are means of resisting this idolatrous situation. We live in extraordinary times, in a world on the brink of nuclear disaster and in a world in the midst of famine. While the weapons of mass destruction are being stockpiled, the mountains of food in the privileged west grow higher. In such times, we are called to extraordinary means to witness to justice, to call our nation and others back from the brink of destruction, to preach the Good News to all people. These means include non-violent direct action and civil disobedience.

CONFRONTATION?

Christians have been rather selective in their ideas and image of Jesus. The notion we have inherited from the Victorians of 'gentle Jesus, meek and mild' is hardly one that fits in with the angry young man who drove the money-changers out of the temple (Matt. 21.12–13; Mark 11.15–17; Luke 19.45–6; John 2.13–16). Legally the money-changers had every right to be there. Their trade was essential for the smooth running of the temple, enabling currency to be changed and sacrifices to be purchased. For the right to trade they were given licences by the priests. Into this legality comes Jesus, who drives out those who are trading and, according to the account in Matthew's Gospel, overturns the tables (Matt. 21.12–13). In a British court today, this would have constituted a breach of the peace. While Jesus did no physical violence to anyone, his actions could have provoked others, in particular the authorities, who had further cause to seek his arrest and execution.

Many Christians shy away from any type of public action for

peace and justice because of their fear of confrontation. In fact preaching the gospel is about a type of confrontation – not violent confrontation for its own sake, or confrontation that dehumanises the other side. Preaching the gospel is about confronting the powers of this world with the Good News. Until the first Pentecost, the apostles hid indoors for fear that they would end up like their master – dead. The Spirit gave them power and confidence to leave the safety of their homes, to preach, heal and witness in public. It led to them being noticed by the authorities, disobeying commands to cease their work of peace. Many were arrested, imprisoned, even executed. It was through such witness that the gospel was spread; it will be through audacious public witness today that the gospel of peace and justice will also flourish.

Answering Questions
Donald Soper

THE advocacy of Christian pacifism, and in particular its practicality in the political and economic fields, can be undertaken in a number of ways, from the mass meeting to the literary document. There is, in my experience, one particular setting for this activity which I have found effective and above all relevant. It is in the interflow of question and answer. I learned this lesson years ago in the open air. I remember a heckler who complained that Christians were busy answering the questions that nobody was asking. Extravagant as such a criticism may be, as a warning it is pertinent in any attempt to communicate a belief and to advocate its practice. Otherwise, however impressive the argument for non-violence, for example, in the Spirit of Jesus, it may well assume a correspondence in thought and approach between the advocator and the advocatee which in fact is not there.

So I will attempt to offer a contribution to this book made up of actual questions posed to me as I have tried to commend Christian pacifism, particularly in the open air. These questions at least have the merit of actuality. They begin where the questioner is, and not where we assume he ought to be. If the answers are set within a similar area of actuality, they can be convincing, as from time to time, I have found them to be. Here are a few of them:

Q. Isn't Christian pacifism a hopeless ideal and, at best, just wishful thinking? How can it become a practical possibility?

A. Let us start at the right place. Politics is largely the way things happen. The pacifist case must be formulated in moral terms, but it must be translated into political and economic undertakings, such as total disarmament and the repudiation of violence as a means of social change. War is integral to the structure of the nation state and, therefore, world government is the necessary society in which peace can be realised and maintained. The format available for these things is parliamentary, democratic and, in the western world, it is party political. Unless there is no party which by its nature can embrace Christian pacifism, the prospects of such a consummation lie within a particular party, wherein its realisation, though not yet fulfilled, is inherently possible. For me, the Labour Party contains that possibility and in its commitment to socialism (however imperfect) it represents the political instrument with which to fashion the pacifist product. Herein lies the programme which can turn the ideal into actuality.

Q. Would not disarmament in the interests of Christian pacifism mean that Russia (or an aggressor) would overrun and subjugate us? Or, alternatively, to disarm would be to encourage the bully and the assassin?

A. Disarmament is, of course, a risk, but we know the risk that armaments have created over the centuries; until today the nuclear threat is absolutely catastrophic. If you believe in the teaching of Jesus, expressed in the way of the Cross and if that teaching represents God's purpose, then disarmament is not a gamble (even if it were, it is a preferable venture to total destruction); it is the obedience that releases God's power and benevolence to his creation.

Q. Is not absolute pacifism impossible? What about the 'fatted calf' (Luke 15.23) in the parable? Did not Jesus compromise in having meals (of meat) with publicans and sinners?

A. This is the most difficult question to answer. In a fallen world, wherein the doctrine of original sin cannot be ignored, no one is completely free to act in absolute obedience to his enlightened conscience. There is an element of compromise in every human action. Final non-violence can only be reached when the Kingdom of God is realised. Nevertheless, we are free to renounce certain forms of violence. War is one of these, and to be obedient to the non-violence of Jesus can be the bell-wether that can lead us to the elimination of other forms of violence. Christian pacifism is an on-going adventure.

The aforementioned are but brief examples of many which are raised in Hyde Park. The answers are, of course, incomplete and, in practice, will provoke further questions and demand amplification of the answers initially given. In that continuing process lies their especial value.

Let me conclude with a personal experience. In years past, a young New Zealander named David Lange was an adherent of the church of which I had charge. Today he is the committed and courageous Prime Minister of New Zealand. I had the opportunity some time ago to visit him and to appreciate the quality of his Christian discipleship and his increasing commitment to the Prince of Peace. He was generous enough to say that I had something to do with his present faith in the Christian pathway to peace. He had found in the meetings in the open air a 'fellowship of controversy' which had ripened into a deeper 'fellowship of belief' which emerged through the 'question and answer' method of approach to the whole problem of mass violence. In a darkening world, I think of Lange and am encouraged.

Breaking Barriers
Between Nations:
International Workcamps

Jenny Barrett

WORLD peace depends on many factors far removed from our own control as individuals. For example, lasting peace will not be experienced until we have a more just international economic order. However, it would be quite wrong to conclude that the attitudes and perceptions of ordinary people have no effect on international relations. Our prejudices and misconceptions about people of other countries do play a role in promoting and sustaining hostility between nations. This country's 'defence' policy is based on a perceived threat from the Soviet Union. That many British people are willing to see the people of the Soviet Union as 'the enemy' is a symptom of widespread ignorance and fear of a political ideology and way of life different from our own. That same ignorance enables people to support a policy of threatening the Soviet people with mass destruction.

The cause of good international relations can be furthered by practical measures which give individuals the opportunity to learn about people in other countries, which help them to enter imaginatively into their viewpoint on world affairs. There are many examples of positive links between people of different countries, from pen-pals to town-twinning. This section will look in some detail at one example: international work camps.

95

WORKCAMPS

The work-camp movement was conceived in the aftermath of the First World War. It was during this period that both SCI (Service Civil International), of which International Voluntary Service is now the British branch, and Christian Movement for Peace were formed. After the carnage of those years, it was obvious to many that future peace depended on working in all possible ways to encourage a spirit of reconciliation and internationalism. There was also a feeling among some that deeds were more effective than words, and there was of course plenty of reconstruction work to be done in the wake of four years of destruction. International voluntary work – people from different countries coming together to work creatively on a practical project – is a fitting antithesis to war, and it was during the early 1920s that SCI organised the first international work camps in Europe.

From the start, there has also been a link between the voluntary work movement and conscientious objection to military service. For example, between the First and Second World Wars, SCI campaigned for the rights of conscientious objectors to engage in civilian service as an alternative to military conscription, showing by its own actions the effectiveness of practical service. Nowadays the Belgian branch of Christian Movement for Peace has workers who spend their national service with them instead of in the army.

The first international workcamp to take place in Britain was at Brynmawr in South Wales in 1931, organised by International Voluntary Service (IVS). A group of volunteers from several different countries came to Wales to work with local people on a scheme to turn this very depressed coal-mining town into a local centre for recreational pursuits.

IVS has continued to organise work camps in Britain ever since then. Since the Second World War, several other organisations have begun to organise work camps in this country: for example, Quaker Workcamps (starting in 1947), United Nations Association (1955), and Christian Movement for Peace (1962). There are now about a dozen organisations running between them several hundred work camps a year in Britain (although not all the camps are international) and also sending volunteers from this country to work camps abroad.

Nowadays a typical work camp consists of a group of between

ten and twenty volunteers living together for about two or three weeks and working on a common project usually for about thirty-five hours per week. They will be provided with free but basic accommodation (for example, in a church hall or community centre) and money for food, which, as a group, they will have to cook and often buy for themselves. They will be expected to spend the whole duration of the camp living communally; working, eating, making decisions and relaxing together. There are no weekends off!

In the early years, work camps were nearly always concerned with construction work, but now there is an enormous variety of projects. Common areas of work include conservation of the environment, play schemes or provision of holidays for children in deprived areas, work with the elderly or with people suffering from mental illness, work with mentally or physically handicapped people and community action of many kinds. Many of the organisations now also run study work camps, where volunteers combine serious study of an issue with practical work.

The international work camp organisations in this country operate exchanges with their sister branches or with other organisations in other countries, so that there is an international mix of volunteers on work camps in Britain and, conversely, British volunteers can volunteer for work camps abroad. There are established links with East and West European countries, some North African countries, Turkey and North America. International workcamps were originally seen as a socially useful method of promoting reconciliation between nations which had been at war. Their aims nowadays are more complex, but still true to the ideal of promoting peace through international understanding. The following are four major elements in the philosophy behind international work camps.

SERVICE Providing service in an area where it is needed has always been a first criterion in the choice of work camp projects. Work is the central and unifying feature of a work camp, around which everything else is built. This work must be socially useful (and the voluntary labour must not be in competition with paid employment). Unless the volunteers themselves believe in the validity of their work, the whole enterprise is unlikely to be successful. It is also hoped that a work camp will actively engage the local community and have lasting benefits for them, perhaps encouraging long-term local involvement in a project.

GROUP LIVING Besides a common work project, volunteers also have the responsibility of living together as a small community, making decisions together and tolerating and learning from each other's different points of view. A group of strangers from vastly different backgrounds soon learn that the only way to organise their common life is through co-operation and a spirit of openness and compromise. There will, of course, be conflicts, but much can be learnt from their peaceful resolution.

LEARNING Volunteers can learn a great deal in a short time through the work they are doing. For example, many people find their understanding of mental health or physical disability quite transformed by a work camp. On study camps, learning takes place in a more formal way, as themes such as racism, peace, development or east-west relations are studied, usually in combination with related practical or campaigning work.

Equally important, learning takes place at a less overt level. Discussion arises naturally out of the experiences and problems of the group. The local community, too, are involved in this learning process.

INTERNATIONAL UNDERSTANDING Breaking down the barriers between people of different nations has always been a central aim of international work camps. Work camps still foster a spirit of internationalism, both among the volunteers themselves and the host community. Particularly important in this respect are the links with countries outside Western Europe. Workcamps involving East and West Europeans are probably the closest that happen today to the original camps, involving the 'hostile' French and Germans. The task of living together harmoniously and working on a common project *requires* international understanding – and forces people to tackle the problems arising from their different cultures and languages.

Many of the movements organising international workcamps are Christian in their origin and inspiration. It should come as no surprise that followers of Christ have been in the forefront of promoting the ideals of peace and service. However, since work camps aim to bring together people with *different* beliefs and backgrounds, they are equally open to volunteers of any or no religion.

A work camp provides a good opportunity to get to know

people from other countries and to learn about the host country. Volunteers are predominantly between eighteen and thirty, but most organisations have dropped any 'youth' stipulations. Anyone interested in taking part in an international workcamp (most of which take place in the summer), or finding out more, should write to one of the following organisations: Christian Movement for Peace, International Voluntary Service, Pax Christi, Quaker Workcamps, United Nations Association (Wales). Their addresses appear in the back of this book.

Learning about Peace: Schools and Curricula

James O'Connell

IRONICALLY, peace has become a controversial area in the curricula of British schools. Partly the reason is that the subject is new; and it arouses suspicions in a conservative sphere. Partly, also, it is often seen as dominantly concerned with the nuclear issue, on which the two largest British political parties are divided. Yet, in spite of suspicions directed at innovations and doubts focused by allegations of bias, it is hard to argue that schools should not be concerned, whether formally or informally, with peace. For one thing, the society and the world that schools are preparing their pupils for are faced with crucial tasks of peacemaking; and for another, schools themselves in their running need peace.

If schools undertake the study of peace, it is necessary to be clear about the broad nature of peace. St Augustine, in the *City of God* (Book XIX), defined peace as 'the tranquillity of order'. The theme of peace contains two basic elements, one positive and one negative: positively, peace is willing co-operation among persons for social and personal goals; and, negatively, peace implies the absence of violence (in the shape of physical, psychological or moral violence).

In the previous paragraph, the stress has been on the concept of peace. In that sense peace can be understood as a state at which people arrive or hope to arrive. The state of perfect peace in which the lion will lie down with the lamb is a pervasive human ideal. Peace has also to be seen as a process. Involved in any living understanding of peace is a set of attitudes among persons that are dynamic and purposeful, that are ready to carry the costs of the search for peace and that seek to uphold the values of justice and freedom inherent in stabilising peace. Hopkins put well the dynamism of peace:

> . . . and when peace here does house,
> He comes with work to do, he does not come to coo,
> He comes to brood and sit.

Peace is, however, flanked by justice and freedom; and peace may well have to live from time to time in some tension with the implications of these latter ideas. Justice requires that everybody and every group receive their due. Freedom involves persons being able to be themselves and, in reasonable measure, to choose their own future. Peace is threatened where justice is not available; and peace is diminished where freedom is denied. The strains on peace in contemporary South Africa, for example, are evident as black Africans resent injustice and protest against lack of freedom. In the work of peace, it is crucial, then, to seek to structure peace with justice and to leaven it with freedom.

CURRICULUM MAKING: PEACE AS A COURSE AND PEACE AS A FOCUS

In considering teaching about peace in schools, two broad approaches seem appropriate. The first is to assemble courses in which peace is explicitly studied. The second is to endeavour to introduce a peace focus in the standard subjects of the curriculum. Let us look at each approach in turn:

1. PEACE STUDIES COURSES Peace covers a vast area that ranges from the actions of individuals to the maintenance of global society and that includes multiple complexities of human behaviour. However, if peace is to provide the basis for a specific school curriculum (and the curriculum issue itself already raises the problem of differing ages and academic levels), it needs to be broken into manageable parts. The following outline structure – which is far from being the only possible – is put forward here as an approach to curriculum making for peace education. It is obviously meant to be implemented according to the requirements of varying levels in schools.

PHILOSOPHY OF NON-VIOLENCE The broad nature of peace; practical approaches to non-violence; the theory of just war; the role of pacifism; case-studies of non-violent action, including Mahatma Gandhi and Martin Luther King.

INDIVIUAL, FAMILY AND SCHOOL PEACE Psychology of personal peace; conditions of peace in families; school organisation and peace; roles of various groups in school, including teachers and pupils.

NUCLEAR ISSUES Politics, strategy and ethics of nuclear weapons; east-west political relations; security, freedom and justice in relation to peace in a nuclear age.

PEACE AND DEVELOPMENT Development and justice; development and compassion; the uneven allocation of world resources; the process of development and its costs in developing societies; development, changing international relations and the threat to peace.

PROBLEMS OF INDUSTRIALISED SOCIETIES Race and multi-cultural relations; industrial firms, management and worker participation; the issue of social class and national community.

CASE-STUDIES Northern Ireland, Central America, the Middle East.

Two further comments are appropriate. First, the contents sketched here can be covered over several years and can be approached according to the ages and needs of school classes. Second, abstract categories and values are best dealt with by being incorporated into case-studies that put flesh and blood on them for young persons.

2. PEACE FOCUS For several reasons, a peace focus in standard subjects is more important than the introduction of peace studies courses. First, it avoids further pressure on overloaded school curricula and yet reaches the attention of a great proportion of pupils. Second, it introduces peace issues more naturally and relevantly into studies. Third, it enriches subjects such as religious knowledge and history which can hardly be taught without a peace focus, as well as subjects such as English and physics which greatly benefit from the focus.

RELIGIOUS KNOWLEDGE Central in religious approaches is a belief that the relations of men and women to God are one side of a coin, of which the other side is their relation to one another. Where a concept of creation is accepted, the fundamental unity

of all persons – Jew and Greek, bond and free, male and female,
Russian and American, European and African – is accepted. In
other words, there is a common humanity which can be
respected only in an ethic of justice and love. This common
humanity is harmed by division; and it is warped by stereotypes.
Beyond basic forms of justice and love, Christian theology
reflects on teachings that propound how enemies have to be
loved and injuries forgiven; how the face that has been struck on
one cheek turns the other cheek (Matt. 5.39); and how with one
who obliges one to go a distance, one goes, voluntarily, a greater
distance (Matt. 5.41). Theologians are under no obligation to
pretend that historically religions, not least Christianity, have
lived up to their ideals. But the ideals can be suggested and their
doctrinal foundations uncovered. At the same time, students
may be invited to discuss why churches, for example, at different
times have not lived up to their ideals. In this context, the social
class of churchmen and nationalism of their congregations may
be looked at. Students can be asked to match the weight of class
and nation against the strength of religious belonging and to
make their judgements on where their own allegiances lie.
Similarly, if a religion accepts that all peoples are brothers and
neighbours, students may be asked to discuss why problems of
just sharing within nations and between nations still remain
outstanding. Finally, it can be suggested that where peoples are
brothers and neighbours, demonisation of leaders or of peoples is
inconsistent with an acceptance that they are the children of
God and open to the Spirit of God. While I have in our present
context used Christianity as my religious example, it is true to
say that, with certain changes, much of what I have said could
be worked out from the foundations of Hinduism and Islam,
while in theologising about the latter two religions it is also
possible to add things that are specific to them. Hinduism, in
particular, has a long history of concern for peace and a record
of having extended peace relations into that part of the world
where men and other animals meet.

HISTORY History taught with a peace concern can point out how
often the study of history is organised around wars. Scholars can
argue the artificiality of such organisation. There may, however, be less need immediately to seek to change the organisation
of data than to sensitise students to the springs of such
organisation. Scholars can also elaborate on the profounder

approaches to periodisation that organise history around social and economic development, the growth of ideas and the introduction and diffusion of technology. In dealing with conflict, it seems sensible to remove romanticism from wars as well as to suggest that most wars have come too soon. In a direct contribution to the analysis of our own period of history, it is useful to examine the stereotypes of one another that opposing peoples have tended to invent before and during wars all throughout history.

ENGLISH The war poets and writings of Huxley and Orwell provide direct ideas for reflection in the teaching of English. They raise the issues of violence and totalitarian control, as well as utopian aspirations and the wreck of hope. Shakespeare provides a lot of thought on national sentiment, especially in a play like *Richard II* where words like 'land' and 'tongue' sound the new Elizabethan sense of national identity. It is also Shakespeare who in *Coriolanus* offers a contrast of personal and social values in the context of war. One way or another, the spectre of death peers into the work of the great poets, Donne and Hopkins not least, who meditate on mortality in great language. What reflections on the death of humanity itself work through contemporary poets as they contemplate the possibility of nuclear disaster and how are previous intimations of mortality taken up?

PHYSICS Physics can show how nuclear weapons have come from a long history of scientific discovery and that the bomb arose out of one of the central efforts of modern physics to split the atom. Moreover, the technology now locks in with solid-state physics, which is currently one of the fastest developing parts of physics. The atomic bomb itself arose out of warfare in an industrial civilisation and was directed against cities. Nuclear bombs, as well as nuclear technology, are, however, part of scientific developments that are gradually modifying nineteenth-century urban growth. Students may be invited to reflect on these developments; and they may also be invited to examine nuclear technology and nuclear weapons as priorities within the comparative priorities of physical science as well as reflect on the implications for the use of the world's resources. There are no easy answers to the questions raised which take in national security as well as the consumption of non-renewable sources of energy. Students of physics are likely, however, to pursue their discipline in a social and economic vacuum unless they, at least, know that there are fundamental questions to be raised in the nuclear area of their discipline as well as analogous questions in other parts of the discipline and in other physical and biological sciences.

Two further comments may be added here. First, the suggestions made above are far from definitive and are best put forward in an illustrative sense only. Second, there is real challenge for teachers and pupils in discussing and working out together possibilities of a peace focus and the place of peace issues in various subjects.

ACTIVE PARTICIPATION

Learning about peace has a crucial intellectual dimension. Yet it is an area where practical learning plays an indispensable role. First, in working together pupils learn the worth of co-operation. Such co-operation can emerge in activities that range from classroom behaviour to organised games. It may also be remembered that so often learning is presented in the school as an individual accomplishment, whereas post-school work has mostly to be collaborative. In this connection, too, the growth of projects where children actively put knowledge together or achieve a practical result fits in with the process of peace. Second, it is important for teachers and pupils to reflect on the overall organisation and ethos of their particular school. This is not to suggest that peace groups should undertake the pre-sumptuous work of seeking to reform a school. But they benefit – as will their teachers – from enquiring about what they can do about their own roles in the school and their own behaviour. Third, whilst there is a case for fostering peace groups in a school, it is well to remember that peace may remain a relatively abstract idea for children in many schools. For that reason, it is worthwhile for pupils to seek to cross boundaries and offer help in dealing particularly with the deprived and the aged who are to be found in every community.

CONCLUSION

Children are influenced more by their families and societies than their schools. Yet schools play a role in imparting skills, reflecting on values and enhancing socialisation. They widen experience beyond the family and usefully reflect on values too readily received in society. If peace studies, as a set of courses or as a focus, is to succeed it needs to bring to bear on the formation of pupils the rigour of academic and pedagogical discipline. Peace is not a soft option for thinking about or studying. But integrated into every academic approach, whether speculative or practical, there needs to be a conviction of the worth of non-violent social change and resolution of conflict. At any time in history, this approach has been important for the quality of human living, but in our time, it has become crucial for global survival.

Changing the Established Church

John Austin Baker

THE title of this section defines a very precise problem. To understand what that problem is, and what can and cannot be done towards solving it, we need to begin with one or two particular reflections on the idea of 'the Church' and on the differing forms which that idea has taken in history.

There is very little in the New Testament traditions about Jesus to suggest that he ever thought in terms of what we would call a 'church' at all. In only two places in the gospels (Matt. 16.18; 18.17) does the term itself appear, and neither has a strong claim to be considered an authentic record of his actual words. If they are authentic, the Semitic language original behind them would, in any case, imply no more than the religious community or congregation of his followers. Of an elaborately structured institution, such as eventually emerged, there is no hint at all.

It needs always to be borne in mind that Jesus came from a tradition which did not think in terms of separate structures for the sacred and the secular aspects of life. For the Jew, the basic reality was the nation under God. The Law, that is the first five books of both the Jewish and Christian Scriptures, told of the creation of Israel as a distinct entity in world history and of the earliest regulations which governed both the civil and religious affairs of that community. The matter is made crystal clear in the closing verse of Psalm 147: 'He [God] has not dealt so with any other nation, neither have the heathen knowledge of his laws.' The 'heathen' are not just people of a different religious faith, who might as easily be found within Israel as outside it –

the assumption a Christian in a modern state would naturally make – but rather they are 'other nations', for to abandon the faith of Israel was to put oneself outside the political and social group to which one had belonged.

In such circumstances, Jesus' mission has to be seen as a reform or renewal movement within Israel. At that time, Jews in the Roman Empire had a distinctive political identity. Some lived in Palestine in small semi-autonomous states. Far more lived dispersed in other parts of the Empire. But wherever they were found, they enjoyed certain limited, but very real rights to organise their own community affairs and to be regulated by their own laws. They were, in short, a definable political entity, even if very different from that of the apogee of their secular power when Solomon had been king 1,000 years earlier. The crucial fact for Jewish self-consciousness, therefore, was that the religious and the secular communities were one and the same. Hence religious conversion or reform aimed at affecting the whole human society, not at setting up a special organisation of a different kind to offer a distinctive approach to purely religious matters. For a Jew, there were no 'purely religious matters'.

A light is thrown by contrast on this fundamental attitude by the phenomenon of the Essenes of Qumran. Here a group who dissented on what they felt were religious essentials took themselves off to live as an independent society in the deserts by the Dead Sea. By contrast, Pharisees, Sadducees and Zealots, the other main religious groupings, stayed as part of the community, but sought to gain political power within it.

For his own followers, Jesus envisaged neither of these roles. Whatever some of them may have dreamed or hoped, Jesus himself did not, in the view of the majority of modern scholars, aim at political power. Nor, at the other extreme, did he wish them to withdraw from the national life into an exclusive settlement. They were to stay within the community – and bear their witness there.

At the same time, it is clear that he did not for one moment suppose that they would convert the whole nation to their way of life. He foresaw for them poverty, sorrow and persecution in this world, and a future reward in heaven as the only ground for their joy. The prayer he taught them was a prayer fitted to the circumstances only of those who had nothing, who had to ask God for their sustenance, even for the next twenty-four hours, and whose hope lay wholly in the coming of the end of history and the new order of God's perfect kingdom. They would be poor and they would be few. But the truth about God's will for humankind was entrusted to them and the very realm of Satan himself would be unable to stand at their approach.

In no context is this vision made clearer than in that of the question of violence. As we have already seen, the use of force was forbidden to them by Jesus. Yet the evidence is equally firm that Jesus foresaw wars and violence continuing to the end of history. Christians have used these predictions to justify their own participation in violence. If those who take the sword perish by the sword (Matt. 26.52), why should not the second of those swords be wielded by Christian hands? But Jesus was not one to have such confusion and contradiction at the heart of any message of his. The simple answer is that he saw his followers as never being more than a minority within their nation and all the more, therefore, a minority in the world. Despite their preaching of repentance and their example of love, the world would go its own way of fear and hatred and slaughter – and these things would grow worse, indeed, rather than better. Today, when despite the fact that more people than ever before are concerned for peace, the number of those who have died in war and violence has reached unimagined heights, that prophecy has been terribly vindicated.

In the early centuries of the Church's history, despite astonishing growth in numbers and extent, the pacifist or non-violent ideal was able to sustain itself because the Church still retained two marks of the condition Jesus wanted for his followers. It was a minority and it was persecuted. In that situation, loyalty to the Lord's teaching was reinforced by the very human, but rather less admirable feelings of spiritual élitism and a corresponding contempt for the beliefs and conduct of those in power. But all this was overthrown by the astonishing reversal under Constantine (d.337). It was not simply the acquisition of power and the incorporation into the state structures which had this effect. There was also the undertow, psychologically all the stronger for being unsuspected, of being now accepted. When those whom you have feared – and perhaps secretly envied and admired – suddenly welcome you into their company, the pressure to accept their values and conform to their practices becomes almost irresistible.

Ever since, the Church has shown itself torn between the various models offered to it by its own history. The call of Jesus' original vision has never lost its power. Either in the diverse forms of the religious life within the Church or in bodies that have broken away from it to realise a greater loyalty to the gospel that vision has been kept alive. But it has also had an indirect and weakened influence on the larger mainstream churches and on their ordinary discipline. Some effort has been made to restrict violence on the part of Christians, or to modify its exercise; and the challenge of the pacifist alternative has never been successfully or for long argued away.

This history gives us valuable pointers towards the possible ways of handling our problem. First, we need to note the ambiguity of the phrase 'established Church'. It may denote any of a number of different situations. Christianity may be the official religion of a nation, sharing in all the perquisites of power and exercising a real influence on its affairs. This influence will not be that of a radical, gospel Christianity, but it may be genuine nevertheless, as many instances from nineteenth-century Britain can show. Or it may be the official religion of the state, but reduced to little more than a bureaucratic 'Department of Religious Belief', tied as to what it can say or do by the prevailing secular ethos – as, some would say, in Sweden today. Again the Church (or the churches between them) may enjoy the relatively active membership of a majority of the population, as in Poland. Or, by contrast, as in Britain today, that membership may be only 9 per cent of the people, despite the fact that Christianity is still the official religion. Each of these situations calls for a different approach.

The next lesson of history is that for those churches whose membership includes a significant percentage of those in positions of power, it is very difficult indeed to stand effectively against the values and policies of government. Perhaps the capacity of the Catholic Church in Poland to resist even a totalitarian régime derives not just from its massive popular base, but also from the fact that those in supreme power are not believing or practising members. In South Africa, however, the Reformed Church is weakened not only by the active membership of those in power, but by the sense that to oppose their policies would be to betray those of one's own kin and culture group in the face of their enemies. In Britain, the Church of England as a whole finds it hard going to maintain 'critical solidarity' with government, not just because many 'establishment' figures (in the popular sense of that word) are active

Christians, but because in a time of numerical weakness churchpeople are afraid to alienate anyone, and especially those who by their influence may be in a position to harm the Church.

To focus, then, on the churches in Britain generally, and on the Church of England in particular, we discover a number of ironies. As a minority group (less than one-tenth of the total population) we Christians ought to be, in theory, well placed to practise 'gospel dissent', which on the present subject would mean, to follow Jesus' law of non-violence. We would seem to be few enough to be able to shake free of the prevailing worldly ideology and many enough to give each other moral and practical strength. But what makes this impossible is that we are not 'poor'. Socially, educationally, financially and politically we are too largely drawn from the upper half of society. In the terms of Jesus' world, we are not Pharisees (as people like to characterise us) but Sadducees.

The alternative option, one which is in fact integral to Anglican tradition, proves equally impossible to achieve, and that is the ideal of the Christian nation. The old concept of Christendom, the fusion of Church with secular society, evolved in the era of nationalism and religious conflict which went with the Reformation to produce this vision of the nation-state united to worship God in a single Church. This, too, could in theory be a sound biblical ideal, one way of attaining the goal of a human society worshipping God and living by his laws, as distinct from an essentially secular state with a church to look after its citizens' 'religious' needs. The quest for some form of theocratic rule, either through a Christian monarch or through an elected oligarchy, occupied a number of the best minds of the Protestant churches. The Anglican structure, presided over by the sovereign as Supreme Governor of the national Church and covering the whole country with a geographical network of parishes, together with its theological ideal of a 'comprehensive' doctrinal system, aimed at securing concord by an insistence on certain primary beliefs, but liberty on secondary matters, was one attempt at a solution. For various reasons, it did not succeed. The unity of Christians which it sought was not to be had. But more fundamentally, the Church of England found that in any symbiosis with the secular state, it is the practicalities of government which dictate how far the gospel will be observed, not the gospel which shapes the policies of government. This is not as the result of a power conflict in which the

Church is defeated, but simply because a church which includes most of society will at best be half-converted and will actually share the values and assumptions of the secular world.

Today the Church of England, like the owners of a decaying stately home, finds itself struggling to keep up institutional structures and a theoretical position in the state from which the social reality has fled. The rambling and lovely edifice no longer serves the human purpose for which it was constructed. The temptation to put all one's energy into attracting enough visitors to keep the house going as a relic of the past is natural enough and is not always resisted. But more and more, in the local congregations, church members (both clergy and lay) are ignoring the theory of Anglicanism and getting down to the same task as all the other churches, that of converting people to Christ and building up communities of praying, practising and witnessing Christians. Sometimes this leads to a flight from involvement with the affairs of the world, sometimes to a more active commitment to bringing those affairs under God's sway; and this divergence is one of the biggest sources of conflict between Christians in Britain today, not least because government tends to make its feelings known in favour of one side of the argument. But this conflict cuts across denominational boundaries. It is one which Anglicans share with most of their fellow Christians and so, ironically, can strengthen a sense of unity, even if only a unity in common problems. For the other great fact of the present situation is a slow but steady growing together of the Christian churches at the local level and this will in time be reflected in structural change, not least in the place of Anglicanism in national institutions, however disappointing efforts for formal reunion of the churches have so far proved.

What in this situation needs to be done to begin to change the established Church over these issues of peace and violence? First, we need to work even harder towards a church unity which derives not only from doctrinal reconciliations, but also from commitment to gospel living. In a society of many faiths and of none, it is the Christian way of being human, both corporately and individually, which will be the hard edge of the Christian presence, drawing others to the faith on which it is based. Here it needs to be said yet again that the present situation, where each church has its own inadequate organisations for advising it on matters of justice and peace and on other issues in social and personal ethics, where resources for research, thought and action are divided and the same pieces of work are done separately three or four times over, is a scandal. It reduces the quality of the results and, at the same time, deprives them of the collective authority they might otherwise possess.

Second, the churches must accept (and all the more, the more closely they work together) that within their membership there are, and will be unless radical changes take place in British society, sincere and devoted Christians of both persuasions as to the nature of the Church. Some will see it in the light of the Gospels as inevitably a small minority within humankind, committed to an extremism of good as the only adequate weapon against evil, as the yeast in the dough, the lamp on the lamp-stand, the city on the hill, the salt in the food that must not lose its savour. Others, rating human nature perhaps more hopefully, will see the Church as a much more open and diverse community, offering a wide variety of people staging-posts on their journey to God, co-operating for human good with everything that is in harmony with Christ's spirit and generally seeking to support, in a critical but positive and reconciling way, the structures of civilisation, understood as springing ultimately from God's goodness in creation. Both views can claim scriptural support. Neither is going to go away just yet. Those who are concerned for the Christian contribution to peace, as for any other gospel goal, should encourage church members to work through both traditions at once, and to develop mutual respect between them.

Third, therefore – to begin with the first of our two visions of the Church – the Churches officially and corporately should make quite clear the unqualified validity of the pacifist position and its authenticity as one crucial expression of the cross-bearing which Jesus demanded of his disciples. Indeed, it could well be regarded as the central expression of that discipleship, because it is here that Jesus' claim on our loyalty parts most radically and painfully from the values of the world. The challenge of non-violence is supremely the sword that divides. Hence no church worthy of the name can do other than stand behind those who follow this vocation. It is not a question of whether the policies for which such people stand would work if governments adopted them. Governments are hardly likely to adopt them. It is simply that no true Christians dare disown the

Master's explicit command to his followers by dissociating themselves from those who try to obey it to the letter. In Anglican terms, such support would presumably imply at least a resolution of General Synod.

Fourth, turning to the second vision of the Church and its role, there is an urgent need to devote many more human and material resources, much more time, thought and prayer, to the vital work for peace which those Christians who cannot commit themselves to a pacifist position can undertake. It would be untrue and unjust to suggest that Christian peace-building can be carried on only from within that position. There are a thousand tasks for peace which need urgently to be done, which do not require fully pacifist convictions. These tasks, if carried through with determination, also involve taking up the Cross in a way that can be profoundly costly. In *The Church and the Bomb*, there were nineteen recommendations of this kind, all of which sank without trace when the other three politically controversial proposals were defeated. Such work includes, for example, every form of campaign and effort to remove those injustices which create the breeding-grounds of violence by offering apparent justification to the cry that nothing but violence will break the grip of deprivation and oppression. It includes the highly sensitive and dangerous work of uncovering and communicating the truth about the world situation to communities soaked in propaganda, conscious and unconscious. It includes the educational tasks of asking the difficult questions about matters of defence or development policy, and of striving to draw government into the educational debate; or of teaching a people to re-learn its history and the history of the world community, in order to exorcise from its own spirit the myths that make fair and sober judgement impossible. It includes the development of the worldwide Christian network to enable every kind of human contact that can make for peace.

War and violence cannot, alas, be prevented simply by removing or reducing conditions of injustice or ignorance or misunderstanding. They are also the product of evils in the human psyche which will be with us so long as this world endures. It also needs to be recognised that even a pacifist way of life, unless universally accepted, cannot prevent violence. It can only limit it by refusal to retaliate. The building of God's kingdom requires commitment to the whole range of peace-making and peace-building activities, of which some few examples have just been given. It will be by starting seriously on tasks across this entire range and calling to each those Christians who can give themselves heart and soul to that particular service, that we shall begin to change such a mixed and manifold body as an established church must always be.

4

A

A GLIMPSE OF

HEAVEN

Just a glimpse . . !

Angelic Interlude
Sara Maitland

I'M not quite sure why I'm telling you this story as a matter of fact. I don't really know what the point of it is. In fact it's a bit silly. But then lots of things are really. Sometimes they're worth telling and sometimes not. Anyway it's about something that happened to me the other day in my sitting room, about halfway between lunch and when the children get in from school.

I was sitting there reading quietly when I heard the all too familiar tones of my guardian angel:

'What in God's name is *that*?'

I suppressed a sigh of irritation. I don't know if I've ever told you about my problems with my guardian angel. The thing is that while most people seem to have completely unintrusive spiritual guides who keep themselves to themselves and even try and disguise their presence, depending entirely on more oblique management techniques (dialectical materialism, or astrology, or evolution, or what have you), mine, presumably because she's too thick for such subtleties, prefers the direct assault. She's always butting in and interrupting my fine thoughts. What's more, while I'm not *unique* in having an interfering angel, I am, so far as I know, unique in having one who is almost unbelievably stupid. She's also rather dumpy and extremely plain, though now I'm a feminist with a raised consciousness I try not to comment on this too much. What's more, she is dead boring: I mean not like Joan's who presented her with mystical voices and led her off to battle and encouraged her to wear drag and command nations and fixed her up with a white horse and a banner and a romantic, if rather painful, death. Most people that I've talked to seem to have heavenly guardian angels who are radiantly beautiful, spiritually profound, intellectually stimulating and even a bit sexy. Quite frankly, mine is the sort who, if she were material, would have halitosis and wear exercise sandals, or something else equally grotty. Once, in a moment of some anger, I asked her if she were God's punishment on me for being an uppity feminist, but of course she completely failed to grasp my heavy irony (have you ever noticed how literal angels are?) and said with her usual tedious but supernatural patience, 'Oh, no, no, no. She doesn't mind *that* at all; what really puts her out is that whenever you buy doughnuts for the children, you always get the ones with loose sugar instead of the glazed kind they really like best.' As I hadn't even noticed that the kids preferred glazed doughnuts, and also realised in a twinkling that I should have noticed; and that, moreover, it is only me who really likes the sugary ones and I don't even eat them being on an ideologically-unsound diet, I was rather peeved. I mean it is much more fun to have a God who disapproves of your politics than a God who prods you about your petty, and in this case purely imaginative, gluttony.

Anyway, to get back to the point, if there is one: that's the sort of guardian angel I've got and I do think it's unfair. So you shouldn't be surprised that I felt some considerable annoyance when she barged in on my quiet moment, saying in her slightly nasal voice,

'What in God's name is *that*?'

'I'm reading,' I said discouragingly.

'I know,' she said, 'But I didn't ask what you were doing, I asked what that was.' One of her rays illuminated the picture on my page.

'Nothing much,' I muttered embarrassed, 'I mean nothing that would interest you, nothing spiritual.'

'Tut-tut,' she said (or however you spell that little noise of disapproval that those sorts of people make), 'You never seem to realise how much we *like* the material. Much more than you lot like the spiritual, you know. What is it?'

I knew it would be difficult to explain. The fact is I was studying this catalogue and trying to decide if I could afford a tiny – I mean really small – a little bitty nuclear bomb. I wasn't going to use it or anything. I mean I'm not the aggressive person around here. I just thought it might be useful to have around, just in case. But I knew she wouldn't like it. She's really wet.

'It's a bomb', I said a bit sullenly.

'A what?' she said.

'Well, like a firework; it goes off with a big bang and makes a cloud of smoke and a bit of a stink',

'Sounds like someone I know', she said thoughtfully, 'What's it for?'

'Nothing much. 'It's a sort of status symbol. I suppose you could use it to make bad people behave themselves and things like that. If they were dangerous.'

'You mean *kill them*?' she sounded amazed. And then I heard a distinctly snuffly sound. *I'm* amazed for that matter that heaven doesn't fix sinusitis, but lets all these adenoidal angels rush round making a nuisance of themselves. Sometimes I really do wonder if God has a clue.

'Look,' I said exasperated, 'I'm not planning to use it or anything. But you're always telling me I don't think about the kids enough and I just thought it would be safer for them if we had one about the house, you know.'

Silence.

'Only in self-defence of course. If everyone was decent I wouldn't want one. But as it is, well I mean if people knew I had one they wouldn't attack me would they? Or the kids of course.'

Silence.

'It's no different from judo classes, is it?' She is always trying to get me to stop smoking and take more exercise and one of her more recent brilliant schemes is that I should go to some women's self-defence class and learn judo, like some bloody Girl Guide. So I thought I'd got her there.

'Women enjoy judo classes,' she said.

'So?'

'So that's the difference. Judo is fun; owning a pet bomb and boasting about it to the neighbours isn't. Or shouldn't be.' I told you she was stupid.

Then there was a long pause. I tried to pretend she'd gone away, but she hadn't. She was hovering somewhere behind my left cortex and looking pained. I just knew she was.

'Sometimes,' I said firmly, and with quite a lot of patience loaded in my expression, 'lacking the supernatural advantages that you lot are lucky enough to possess, you just have to play on their terms. If you're weak, they won't respect you, they might hurt you and they certainly won't listen to you. You need influence. Even Simone Weil used to say that you had to have prestige, as much prestige as they did.' Simone Weil, as I well knew, had not meant exactly that at all, but I felt I could count on my angel not knowing this fact.

Silence.

Not the sort of silence that meant she was thinking about it; the sort that meant she was expecting me to think about it. Suddenly, I had this brilliant idea, fighting fire with fire it's called. 'Even you lot go in for it sometimes. What about when you threw the forces of Satan out, huh? War in heaven? Apocalypse now, eh? You can't be passive or pacifistic in the face of evil, can you?'

There was another pause. I thought she was in retreat. I pressed my advantage.

'Come on,' I crowed, 'don't duck. If heaven is allowed wars, why aren't we?'

'I don't know if I should tell you this,' she said quietly, 'God knows what use you'll make of it, but actually we used trampolines.'

'Trampolines!' I yelled.

'Sure. Trampolines. They really are defensive.' You can have one of them if you like. They're fun, like judo.'

I was indignant. Outraged actually. And incredulous.

'Look', she said, 'It's very simple. You set up a line of trampolines and if people want to charge around, they just bounce off. They bounced a long way I admit, poor snakes, but that was mostly our fault because we didn't really understand about gravity. It was before the creation. I expect She was still experimenting. They know they can come back any time they want to play. They're just sulking, that's all. We laughed so much.'

Trampolines. At Christmas time in the trenches of the First World War, both sides played football together; then they hopped back in their trenches and charged each other. A few trampolines might have been a neat idea.

But I was still taken with the idea of having my own bomb. Hardly anyone had got one after all. And this one was a real bargain, relatively speaking. I realised that if I let her know I was impressed by trampolines, she'd take an unfair advantage. I had to fight on now to defend myself for having started. I tried a new line of attack:

'Trampolines. I don't believe a word of it. Anyway, what about St George?'

'Good heavens,' she exclaimed, 'I thought you of all people ought to know that all that was just an early medieval co-option of a variety of pagan stories, typical mythopoeic structure.' I ask you. It simply was not fair: the last thing you anticipate from angels is demystification. Especially when they're stupid.

'OK. OK.' I intervened quickly. I had no intention of being forced onto the defensive. 'St Michael then. Angelic? Right? Biblical, too. You can't get out of that one.' I nearly said, 'So there', like a child, but caught myself just in time.

'Michael,' she said bewildered.

'Yeah. Michael. You know, the archangel.'

'Yes, of course I know', she said, 'but what does that have to do with anything?'

I had a moment of pure triumph, I could almost afford to be generous to the vanquished; almost. 'You cheat', I cried delightedly, 'Come on. Devil slaying? Fully armed – to the hilt, if a poor mortal is allowed a joke. Long spear? You know.' Oh, I was pleased with myself and my crushing victory. Game, set and match to me I thought with relish.

'Spear!' she said, 'Spear? Is that what you think? Unbelievable.'

'Surrender,' I taunted.

'That's not a spear, you silly little girl, that's a tickle stick.' And after a long pause she said with great tenderness, 'Oh poor Michael.'

'Poor Michael?' I said, slightly put out. I have to admit that she had put a shot right across my bows. And she had never spoken to me in that loving tone.

'The poor love', she continued. 'Listen to me, you absolutely must not tell. Michael would be so upset. And it's so unfair. We thought the tickle stick would be such fun for him, a sort of reward or consolation, because of Gabriel getting the best job you know. And you all think it's a spear. Oh dear. You are so silly.'

'Silly!' And here was she practically blubbing over some angel and a bit of tickling apparatus.

'Yes, silly. Stupid. Poor Michael, how embarrassing', she continued.

'Embarrassing.' 'He really spends eternity running around like some tiresome little girl in the playground, while everyone thinks he has a decent part to play: pig-sticking Lucifer, and that wonderful statue at Coventry and those beautiful Russian paintings. I wouldn't be complaining.'

'No, well you probably wouldn't', she said. 'Oh, I'm fed up with you; you're so boring and stupid I sometimes wonder if you're God's punishment on *me* for being such a chatterbox. Here's Michael skipping round heaven making everyone happy and being so generous and gentle and lovely about letting Gabriel announce the Prince of Peace and having all the attention. And humanity use him as an excuse for killing each other. I'd die of shame if it were me.'

'But he's a hero.'

'Exactly', she replied, 'That's why I'd die of shame.'

She looked so tragical that I felt as though she'd lost and I'd won. I couldn't even feel pleased about it.

'Look,' I said quite suddenly, nearly surprising myself, 'I won't buy the bloody bomb; I never wanted it anyway.' She wasn't very grateful, considering that I was making this sacrifice just to cheer her up. 'I should think not indeed', she said, like a prissy nanny.

She began to dissolve, sinking faintly down into my lower left cranial cavity as usual, preparatory to flowing away into my spinal fluid. 'Peace be with you', she said as she always did on departure, trite to the end.

And then she tickled me. Having your brain tickled is ecstatic. It's not a mystical experience actually, it's more sort of, well, fun. I just caught a fading glance of her cheerful grin and peaceable nose, and do you know, just for that moment it did seem to me that she was spiritually profound, radiantly beautiful and even a little bit sexy.

5

CONCLUSION

In which the end is but the beginning . . .

Peace at the Last
Clive Barrett

A VISION OF HOPE

WHEN Evelyn Underhill wrote the Postcript to an APF book *Into the Way of Peace* (1941), she described pacifism as 'a positive and creative direction for living'. In *Peace Together*, we have seen the roots of this direction for living in the Christian Scriptures, theology and practice. Peacemakers, old and young, have shown the ways of war to be evil means which cannot cast out evil. Many, in a nuclear age, have realised that there can be no greater evil than nuclear war, bringing unthinkable global consequences. In an age of deterrence, the unthinkable becomes thinkable. Deterrence is surely hell – that spiritual wasteland created by the idolatry of national security, by putting ultimate trust in the infallibility of human technology and the control of human nature.

Has any weapon ever been invented without being used? (How the arms manufacturers rejoice when there is war in the 'two-thirds' world.) Nuclear weapons cannot be disinvented. There is need for repentance, a turning from policies which have *always* failed. Pacifists fully recognise the fallibility of human nature and we realise that the world's arsenals of nuclear, chemical and biological weapons *will be used* unless dramatic initiatives are taken towards disarmament. As one former soldier converted to pacifism testifies, 'I am a pacifist *because* I am a desperately violent man.' The need for repentance is urgent. *Now* is the time for turning to that 'positive and creative direction for living.'

Pacifist Christians hold out hope for the future. The renunciation of war and its preparation, and the working for the construction of world peace can bring true and realistic hope to the world. There have been signs of hope even in the twentieth century: the non-violence of Mahatma Gandhi and Martin Luther King, inspiration for people of all faiths; the spirituality of Thomas Merton and the witness of Martin Niemöller ('Because I was an ecumenist I became a pacifist.'); white conscientious objectors to military service in South Africa (including APF members); the courage and persistence of Christian peace movements across the world. What is more, the gospel is a message of hope. Only if our proclamation is true to the gospel, will it be heard and responded to by others. The need for Christians to embrace the vision of pacifism has never been greater for our church and our world.

We go forward in prayer and in hope. Cardinal Suenens once wrote about life in the Holy Spirit:

> To hope is a duty not a luxury.
> To hope is not a dream, but to turn dream into reality.
> Happy are those who dream dreams and are ready to pay the price
>   to make them come true.

POLICIES FOR PEACE

Our dreams are capable of being translated into practical politics. The details of the following suggestions must be subject to debate and negotiation, but the basis for one possible way forward could include:

1 Britain immediately deciding to become nuclear-free (the Soviet Union has agreed to match such a step, weapon for weapon) and to destroy all stocks of biological and chemical weapons.

2 Refusal to belong to any deterrence-based military alliance, such as NATO. Associated with this would be the recall of all British overseas armed forces and the departure from Britain of all American armed forces which occupy dozens of military bases. (A massive step towards international peace will come when all armies remain on their own soil.)

3 The abandonment of any weapons that could be used aggressively, e.g. 'conventional' missiles, long-distance bombers, etc. The removal of threats that create fear in others and promote counter-threats, i.e. 'deterrence'. The remaining

weaponry, e.g. for coastal protection or anti-aircraft use, would at least be able to be honestly termed 'defensive'. The above policies would hasten the day when even these were superfluous.

4 Coincident with these policies, an end to all trade in arms would mean that scientific research and modern technology could be liberated for creativity rather than destruction.

Such a course as this could be associated at each stage with a massive transfer of expenditure from armaments to social provision at home and justice for the poor in the 'two-thirds' world. Not only would such policies spring from right intentions, they would have right consequences. They would break the spiral of destruction and could inspire other nations to follow. In such a climate, even multilateral negotiations for world disarmament could be taken seriously. In an age of overkill, massive disarmament by any nation must be a step in the right direction.

There may be risks in following such policies. The risks in not following them are substantially higher. Over forty years of exporting wars to other continents, of diverting the gifts of creation to the means of destruction have brought us to the point where one small computer error or one mad president could signal the end. Did Christ die for this?

LIVING THE KINGDOM

We cannot leave it up to God. We have been created with the free will to choose God or to choose evil. God does not protect us from our choice. God will not pluck missiles out of the sky to protect us from nuclear doom.

We must trust in God and in the power of love. We know that in choosing God we will be used by him to bring about his peace. A prayer of St Teresa reminds us 'Christ has no hands but your hands to do his work today.' The 'Prayer of St Francis' asks, 'Lord, make me an instrument of your peace.' The way of peace, rooted in prayer, will be different for each of us. Many will join campaigning and witnessing organisations. (As well as national groups listed in Appendix 1, there are various local Christian peace groups throughout the country. There is an APF membership form in Appendix 2.) Many will respond to the words of Evelyn Underhill: 'The pacifist, then, must be content to begin where he is. . . . The home, the street, the workplace, the city should be his first, perhaps his only sphere.'

We are to pray, think, speak, act peace in our daily lives. We can even play peace (no war toys for our children!).

Thomas Merton warns about quietism, but he adds that it is ' "fighting for peace" that starts all the wars. Peace is something you have or do not have. If you yourself are at peace, then there is at least *some* peace in the world.'

It is no surprise, then, that a 'Universal Prayer for Peace' is part of the spirituality of many people across the world. It sums up the pacifist hope. Make it your own:

> Lead me from death to life, from falsehood to truth.
> Lead me from despair to hope, from fear to trust.
> Lead me from hate to love, from war to peace.
> Let peace fill our heart, our world, our universe.
> Peace. Peace. Peace.

Appendix 1
Useful Addresses

Anglican Pacifist Fellowship, St Mary's Church House, Bayswater Road, Oxford OX3 9EY. Tel. 0865-61886.

Anti-Apartheid Movement, 13 Mandela Street, London NW1. Tel. 01-387 7966.

Campaign Against the Arms Trade, 11 Goodwin Street, London N4 3HQ. Tel. 01-281 0297.

Christian Campaign for Nuclear Disarmament (also CND), 22–4 Underwood Street, London N1 7JG. Tel. 01-250 4010.

Christian Movement for Peace, Bethnal Green United Reformed Church, Pott Street, London E2 0EF. Tel. 01-729 7985.

Clergy Against Nuclear Arms, 38 Main Road, Evesham, Worcs. WR11 4TL. Tel. 0386-870918.

Corrymeela Community, Ballycastle, County Antrim, Northern Ireland. Tel. 02657-62626.

Fellowship of Reconciliation, 40–6 Harleyford Road, London SE11 5AY. Tel. 01-582 9054.

Greenpeace, 36 Graham Street, London N1 8LL. Tel. 01-608 1461.

International Voluntary Service (for work camps), Ceresole House, 53 Regent Road, Leicester LE1 6YL. Tel. 0533-541862.

Pax Christi, St Francis of Assisi Centre, Pottery Lane, London W11 4NQ. Tel. 01-727 4609.

Peace News, 8 Elm Avenue, Nottingham NG3 4GF. Tel. 0602-503587.

Peace Pledge Union, Dick Sheppard House, 6 Endsleigh Street, London WC1H 0DX. Tel. 01-387 5501.

Peace Tax Campaign, 1A, Hollybush Place, London E2 9QX. Tel. 01-739 5088

Quaker Peace and Service (also Quaker work camps), Friends House, Euston Road, London NW1 2BJ. Tel. 01-387 3601.

United Nations Association, 3 Whitehall Court, London SW1A 2EL. Tel. 01-930 2931.

UNA Wales (for work camps), Welsh Centre for International Affairs, Temple of Peace, Cathays Park, Cardiff CF1 3AP. Tel. 0222-28549.

Week of Prayer for World Peace, Centre for International Peacebuilding, Wickham House, 10 Cleveland Way, Mile End Road, London E1 4TR. Tel. 01-790 2424.

World Development Movement, Bedford Chambers, London WC2E 8HA. Tel. 01 836 3672.

Appendix 2
APF Membership Form

ANGLICAN PACIFIST FELLOWSHIP

'We, communicant members of the Church of England, or of a Church in full communion with it, believing that our membership of the Christian Church involves the complete repudiation of modern war, pledge ourselves to renounce war and all preparation to wage war, and to work for the construction of Christian peace in the world.'

I am in full agreement with the above declaration and wish to become a member.

Name (Rev., Mr, Mrs or Miss) ....

(Please print clearly CHRISTIAN NAMES & SURNAME)

Address ....

....

I enclose £   as my first subscription. (There is no fixed subscription. Members are asked to give as liberally as they can.)

Diocese ....

Our newsletter *Challenge* is the chief means by which members are kept in touch with the Fellowship. It is sent to all subscribing members unless they request otherwise. All who are able are asked to include in their subscription an additional amount to cover the cost of *Challenge*.

If you are able to sign a deed of covenant for your subscription, so that we can recover the Income Tax that you pay on it, please put a tick here and DO NOT SEND YOUR SUBSCRIPTION till you have received the Deed to sign.

I suggest an explanatory leaflet be sent to ....

....

(Tick or delete the following as required)
Please send APF badge (40p post paid)
I would also like to receive information about the Fellowship of Reconciliation

To the Hon. Secretary,
ANGLICAN PACIFIST FELLOWSHIP
St Mary's Vicarage,
Bayswater Road, Headington, Oxford OX3 9EY

Year of Birth ....
Date ....
Signed ....